Mary Wollstonecraft:
An Annotated Bibliography

Garland Reference Library in the Humanities (Vol. 36)

Mary Wollstonecraft:
An Annotated Bibliography

Janet M. Todd

Garland Publishing, Inc., New York & London

1976

Library of Congress Cataloging in Publication Data

Todd, Janet M   1942–
  Mary Wollstonecraft : an annotated bibliography.

  (Garland reference library in the humanities ; v. 36)
  Includes index.
  1. Wollstonecraft, Mary, 1759–1797—Bibliography.
Z8981.5.T62 ₍PR5841.W8₎ 016.828'6'09   75–24095
ISBN 0–8340–9976–1

Printed in the United States of America

Contents

Frontispiece (Mary Wollstonecraft, by John Opie. Reprinted by permission from the Tate Gallery, London)

JAN 7 1981

Preface

In spite of the two centuries of interest in Wollstonecraft, this is the first comprehensive annotated bibliography of her works and criticism. It is designed both as a research tool for scholars and students and as a revelation of the quantity and variety of comment. It suggests the vagaries of Wollstonecraft's posthumous reputation and indicates the peaks and troughs of interest.

The bibliography includes works by Wollstonecraft, as well as most of the critical and biographical comment on her in English written between 1788 and 1975. Most book reviews are listed, except in cases where they evaluate studies of Wollstonecraft while making little reference to her. Editions and collections of Wollstonecraft's works are included only when they have original prefatory material. There are several foreign-language items, but the bibliography is by no means intended as inclusive in this area.

Books are listed under their authors' names; where the author is unknown, the book is listed under its title. If the comment on Wollstonecraft occurs in an essay within a longer work, the item is listed under the name of the author of the comment, not the name of the editor or compiler of the work. Where an edition of Wollstonecraft is published with an introduction, it is listed under the name of the introducer.

The bibliography is divided into three main sections. The first lists items from 1788 to 1799; the second those from 1800 to 1899, and the third those from 1900 to the present time. The choice of section depends on the publication date of the work used for annotation. A short section of addenda includes a few items either recently obtained or recently published.

In the eighteenth-century section, reviews and articles occur under the title of the journal in which they appear, since most of such items are anonymous. In the nineteenth- and twentieth-century sections, anonymous reviews continue to be

PREFACE

listed under the titles of the journals, but signed items are placed under their authors' names.

The bibliography was compiled primarily at the Douglass and Alexander Libraries of Rutgers University and at the New York Public Library. Several outstanding items were discovered at the British Museum Library in London. Still others were obtained from various American libraries through the interlibrary loan services of Douglass College. I am indebted to Anne Brugh for her help in tracing many of these items.

The preparation of this bibliography has been advanced in many ways by the assistance and interest of others. First of all, I am very much indebted to Burton R. Pollin whose *Godwin Criticism: A Synoptic Bibliography* has been an example both daunting and encouraging. Many items in this bibliography refer to Wollstonecraft and in several cases, where I have not been able to trace the reference, I have listed the item with attribution to Pollin's work. The number following his name is the number of the item in *Godwin Criticism*. The critical introduction to Wollstonecraft first appeared in *British Studies Monitor;* I am grateful to Roger Howell, Jr. for his permission to reprint it here.

I owe thanks to Takako Shirai for the Japanese items; these are useful in suggesting the widespread interest in Wollstonecraft in recent years. I am grateful, also, to Gloria Cohn for typing the manuscript and to Catherine Dammeyer for proofreading much of it.

My main debt of gratitude is to Susan Riccio. She has contributed several items to the bibliography and found many more. She has actively participated in all stages of the compilation and has been a constant source of support in days of bibliographical dejection.

Critical Introduction

In 1792, Mary Wollstonecraft published her *Vindication of the Rights of Woman.*[1] Several eighteenth-century women before her, such as Mary Astell, "Sophia," and Catherine Macaulay, had written on women, their rights and their education, but Wollstonecraft fired a generation of women with her ideas in a way her predecessors had not. This was partly due to the time when she wrote, during the early part of the French Revolution, when many radical writers in England were discussing human rights and education, and so were preparing the public for Wollstonecraft's feminist ideas. It was also due to her welding of personal experience with theory, which gives conviction and passion to her work. It is not surprising, then, that her work and her life should both have attracted attention; indeed the life has exerted such a powerful compulsion that the majority of comments on Wollstonecraft, both in her own time and later, have been biographical.

LETTERS

The torrential quality of Wollstonecraft's life is most apparent in her letters. The life revealed in the letters is remarkably full, for the long agony of the Imlay relationship is recorded, often created, on paper, and even the satisfactory and finally marital relationship with Godwin proceeded largely in this way. We thus have a record that strikes us with an impact rarely made by a biography, an impact so great that undoubtedly Wollstonecraft's letters are among her greatest creative works.

The letters occur in many modern collections that frequently overlap. William Godwin first published Wollstonecraft's personal letters to Imlay in his *Memoirs of the Author of "A Vindication of the Rights of Woman."*[2] These letters were reprinted a century later by C. Kegan Paul and, later still, by Roger Ingpen.[3] In 1937, Benjamin P. Kurtz and Carrie C.

Autrey printed letters from Wollstonecraft in *Four New Letters of Mary Wollstonecraft and Helen Maria Williams.*[4] The letters of Wollstonecraft to Godwin occur in Godwin's work, in Ralph Wardle's biography, *Mary Wollstonecraft: A Critical Biography,* and in Wardle's *Godwin and Mary: Letters of William Godwin and Mary Wollstonecraft,* which prints some new letters and some previously published inaccurately by C. Kegan Paul in his *William Godwin: His Friends and Contemporaries.*[5]

Two other works have substantial numbers of Wollstonecraft letters. The first is W. Clark Durant's Supplement to his edition of Godwin's *Memoirs of Mary Wollstonecraft;* in this the letters are given in full and placed within the context of Wollstonecraft's life.[6] The other is Kenneth Neill Cameron's *Shelley and His Circle,* an edition of manuscripts of the Shelley and Godwin-Wollstonecraft circles.[7] The introductions and placings of the documents in this work are excellent, and indeed certain episodes of Wollstonecraft's life emerge more fully and more strikingly here than in the biographies, where they are treated summarily or submerged in the general welter of the life. An example is the friendship of Wollstonecraft with Henry Gabell recorded in the letters of Volume IV.

Other letters from Wollstonecraft are scattered over various volumes. Several of the most important collections have not yet been found, or, as in the case of the Fuseli letters, have presumably been destroyed. Most of the discovered letters are now easily available, but the number of works over which they range is a hindrance to their study. All students of Mary Wollstonecraft must therefore welcome Ralph Wardle's decision to edit a complete set of the letters.

WORKS

Wollstonecraft's first major polemical work, *A Vindication of the Rights of Men,* has been reproduced in facsimile, with an introduction by Eleanor Louise Nicholes.[8] The facsimile edition is of great importance since it copies a very scarce work, interesting for its own sake and for an understanding of its more famous successor, *A Vindication of the Rights of Woman.* In her introduction, Nicholes stresses the conceptual relationship of the two *Vindications,* and she briefly provides an historical framework useful for both works. She finds in Wollstonecraft's life an intellectual movement toward the Dissenting philosophy of Dr. Price with its emphasis on justice, democracy, and popular liberty. More specifically for the *Rights of Men,* she relates the controversy between Edmund Burke and Dr. Price, and emphasizes the relationship of Price's sermon to English rather than French revolutionary events, a relationship that Burke's rhetoric did much to obscure.

A Vindication of the Rights of Woman is at present readily available in Norton library and Penguin editions.[9] The Norton edition follows the text of 1891 by Mrs. Fawcett, although it has been corrected in places to agree with Wollstonecraft's revised text of 1792. There is a short introduction by Charles W. Hagelman, Jr., which chooses to concentrate mainly on *The Rights of Men.* What is most appealing for Hagelman in *The Rights of Woman* is not the originality of Wollstonecraft's ideas or the felicity of their expression, but the devotion to humanity and the concern for its well being. The Penguin introduction by Miriam Brody Kramnick sketches Wollstonecraft's life and briefly discusses her minor works. *A Vindication of the Rights of Woman* is set in its political context of the 1790s and in its historical feminist context of the eighteenth and nineteenth centuries. The main argument of the book is summarized, and Kramnick concludes that it is so comprehensive that one may say that all feminists, radical and conservative, who followed Wollstonecraft are her philosophic descendants. Several facsimile editions also exist of *A Vindication of the Rights of Woman,* and excerpts from it usually occur in feminist anthologies, for example, *Women's Liberation and Literature,* edited by Elaine Showalter, and *The Feminist Papers,* edited by Alice S. Rossi.[10]

Some useful facsimile editions of Wollstonecraft's less famous works have been issued by Garland Publishing, Inc.: *Mary, A Fiction, Posthumous Works,* edited by William Godwin, and *Thoughts on the Education of Daughters.*[11] The introductions, which summarize Wollstonecraft's life and quote some modern critical opinions of the works, are by Gina Luria. Wollstonecraft's last work published in her lifetime,

Letters Written during a Short Residence in Sweden, Norway, and Denmark, has been reproduced by Centaur Press.[12] The introduction by Sylva Norman describes the *Letters* as the most objective and mature of Wollstonecraft's works. Scholars' Facsimiles & Reprints has recently brought out *An Historical and Moral View of the Origin and Progress of the French Revolution;* the introduction by Janet M. Todd relates the history to other contemporary accounts of France and traces the influence on Wollstonecraft's thinking of the cataclysmic events of the later Revolution.[13]

Wollstonecraft's novels are now available in several editions. The most accessible one of *The Wrongs of Woman* is by Norton; its introduction by Moira Ferguson relates the work to Wollstonecraft's life and to the earlier *Vindication of the Rights of Woman,* whose sequel it in many ways appears to be.[14]

The Emigrants, a novel usually attributed to Gilbert Imlay, Wollstonecraft's American lover, is given to Wollstonecraft by Robert R. Hare in his introduction to the facsimile reprint of the work.[15] Hare bases much of his case on the similarity between *The Emigrants* and Wollstonecraft's autobiographical novel, *The Wrongs of Woman,* and he supports it by pointing out several stylistic habits and attitudes common in Wollstonecraft's other works. Hare further considers Wollstonecraft to be the author of *A Topographical Description of the Western Territory of North America,* another work usually attributed to Imlay. This book, which shows little firsthand knowledge of America, is aimed at encouraging immigration and was written at a time when Wollstonecraft's brother, Charles, was planning to emigrate from England. P.M. Pénigault-Duhet, in her article "Du nouveau sur Mary Wollstonecraft; l'oeuvre littéraire de George Imlay," throws some doubt on Hare's thesis.[16] In particular, she questions why Godwin in his *Memoirs* should not have alluded to his wife's authorship of the two books.

Both Hare and Pénigault-Duhet have some merit in their arguments, and the question of the authorship of the "Imlay" books must therefore remain open. Certainly it points to the need for much more investigation of the shifting literary, political, and amorous relationships of the expatriate circle in revolutionary France.

BIOGRAPHICAL AND CRITICAL COMMENT

The main known facts of Wollstonecraft's life are her wandering youth dominated by a weak, tyrannical father, her later care for her family and that of her friend, Fanny Blood, her struggle to earn an independent living, her association with the circle of Dr. Price, her period as governess to the nobility, authorship and the association with the radical thinkers of her publisher's circle, the episode with Fuseli, the period in revolutionary France, the relationship with the American, Imlay, by whom she had a child, the Scandinavian escape as Imlay's business representative, the suicide attempts after proofs of his infidelity, the marriage with Godwin, and the death in childbirth. Although Wollstonecraft's family situation in youth and her early attempts to earn an independent living are probably most formative for her feminist philosophy, it is the associations with Imlay and Godwin that have received most biographical comment. One reason is the visibility of these associations from her letters; another is the contemporary and later obsession with irregular liaisons, together with the desire to prove through their existence the rightness or wrongness of Wollstonecraft's unconventional philosophy.

The notoriety of Wollstonecraft and Godwin after their marriage resulted in several satires and diatribes, some of which have been studied by Burton R. Pollin and Robert E. Loomis. In "The Godwin's [sic] in *The Letters of Shahcoolen,"* Loomis discusses an American work satirizing Wollstonecraft and Godwin.[17] Written as a series of letters to discredit radical ideas and expose their harmful effects in America, this work aims primarily at Wollstonecraft, who is seen waging war against everything feminine. The attack is on Wollstonecraft's character more than her literary works, and it is noteworthy that the facts used must have come from Godwin's *Memoirs,* the earliest biography of Wollstonecraft and notorious in its time for its frankness concerning her unconventional relationships. *The Letters of Shahcoolen* (1802) has been reissued in facsimile with an introduction by Ben Harris McClary.[18] In "A Federalist Farrago," Pollin includes federalist satire on Godwin and Wollstonecraft, and reveals how widespread was the hostility toward their views and public characters.[19]

An English opponent of Wollstonecraft is discussed in another article by Loomis: "The Turning Point in Pope's Reputation: A Dispute Which Preceded the Bowles-Byron Controversy."[20] This concerns J. Mathias, who in *The Shade of Alexander Pope on the Banks of the Thames* makes a resuscitated Pope praise the current government and attack its opponents, among whom is Mary Wollstonecraft. As in *The Letters of Shahcoolen,* there is proof in this work of the hostile reception of Godwin's *Memoirs,* called in a footnote *"The Philosopher's* unblushing account of his own Wife's amours, life, and conduct."

Inspired by Mathias, the Reverend Polwhele provided his own blast against Wollstonecraft in *The Unsex'd Females,* where he sees her death in childbirth almost as a judgment against her perverted femininity and against the philosophy of her life.[21] Polwhele's work and the anti-Wollstonecraft tradition it inspired are the subjects of Janet M. Todd's article, "The Polwhelean Tradition and Richard Cobb."[22] The article identifies a tradition stemming from Polwhele and having as its main twentieth-century exponents Ferdinand Lundberg and Marynia Farnham (1947), who accuse Wollstonecraft of perverted sexuality, and Richard Cobb (1974), who accuses her of malevolence and social destructiveness.[23] Like Polwhele, these modern detractors seem to suggest Wollstonecraft's early death as a culmination of a perverted attempt to turn people from the decencies of life.

Through the nineteenth and twentieth centuries, there have been occasional essays on Wollstonecraft that have testified less to her notoriety than to her appeal. These have usually illuminated more through emotional insight than through factual research. George Eliot, whose reputed relationship with Chapman resembled Wollstonecraft's with Fuseli, chooses to discuss the work rather than the life in an article on Wollstonecraft and Margaret Fuller, written in 1855 and recently reprinted in *Essays of George Eliot.*[24] Eliot finds *The*

INTRODUCTION

Rights of Woman an eminently serious and moral work, and she emphasizes Wollstonecraft's understanding and her rather heavy rationalism. She quotes approvingly Wollstonecraft's opinion that men, horrified at the idea of an intelligence in women that would make them equal to men, are yet frequently subjected to the silly and ignorant women they approve. In addition, Eliot grasps and emphasizes Wollstonecraft's reiterated point, that the subjection of women is also the subjection of men. Unfortunately, Eliot does not continue her study, breaking off with a shrug about her "desultory material."

At the beginning of this century, another famous woman, the anthropologist Ruth Benedict, recorded her reaction to the life and works of Wollstonecraft.[25] Although her short article, reprinted in Margaret Mead's edition of her work, is marred by the restatement of clichéd opinions about Wollstonecraft's life, Benedict does communicate an enthusiasm for her subject. She sees Wollstonecraft as a crusader against privilege of all kinds, and she makes the common analogy between Wollstonecraft's hostile feelings toward her father and her later ones toward the unjustly privileged. The essay is of interest primarily for its revelation of the inspiration Wollstonecraft can be to other exceptional women.

The best of the short sketches by famous women testifying to Wollstonecraft's appeal is that by Virginia Woolf in *The Second Common Reader*.[26] In a few pages of assertions, she conveys the feeling rather than the facts of Wollstonecraft's experimental and thrusting life, and in the process she reveals her own enthusiasm for her subject. She transfixes her insights in memorable images, such as the much quoted one for the Imlay-Wollstonecraft relationship: "Tickling minnows he had hooked a dolphin," an image that conveys both the impression given by Wollstonecraft's letters and the ironic sympathy of Virginia Woolf.

Several recent articles treat in a more scholarly, less impressionistic way various aspects and events of Wollstonecraft's life. George Mills Harper aims to correct a careless observation of W. Clark Durant, an editor of Godwin's *Memoirs,* concerning the date of Wollstonecraft's residence with Thomas Taylor, the Platonist.[27] Harper quotes a favorable opinion of Taylor about Wollstonecraft, and in view of it wonders why Taylor should have parodied *The Rights of Woman* in his *Vindication of the Rights of Brutes*. Elizabeth Nitchie concerns herself with identifying an early suitor of Wollstonecraft. She suggests Joshua Waterhouse, a fashionable clergyman, later turned recluse and miser.[28] In the obituaries after his murder in 1827, there is a mention of several letters of Wollstonecraft, now presumably lost. Nitchie suggests Waterhouse as the original of the unnamed gentleman, whom the heroine of *Mary* meets at a friend's house, a "man, past the meridian of life, of polished manners, and dazzling wit." Waterhouse may also have inspired the passages in *Thoughts on the Education of Daughters* concerning the misery of a woman in love with a man of whom her reason disapproves.

Wollstonecraft's association with Godwin is the subject of an article by Jean Detre in *Ms.*[29] This makes the point that Godwin held essentially sexist views, while admiring his wife's liberated character and ideas. For example, he distinguishes women from men by their lack of reasoning powers. At the same time, the article stresses the courage that both Wollstonecraft and Godwin showed in fighting prejudice against the unconventional in morals and manners. Detre's interest in Wollstonecraft and Godwin has led her to write a part-fictional and part-historical account of their relationship in *A Most Extraordinary Pair*.[30] Detre places beside the letters which Wollstonecraft and Godwin wrote to each other a journal which she imagines Wollstonecraft could have written during the same period.

Several books and articles treat Wollstonecraft within the context of a wider study and so usually retell the life to suit a thesis. D. L. Hobman in *Go Spin, You Jade: Studies in the Emancipation of Woman* (1957) adds to the usual simplified résumé of Wollstonecraft's life a brief discussion of *The Rights of Woman,* whose tone is seen as "curiously modern."[31] Doris Mary Stenton in *The English Woman in History,* written in the same year as Hobman's book, aims to display the place women held and the influence they exerted within the changing pattern of English society.[32] She gives an even more inaccurate account of Wollstonecraft's life than Hobman, and she concludes it by finding Wollstonecraft's work overrated, because she was not the first to draw attention to women's lack of political rights. She indirectly suggests Wollstonecraft's importance, however, when she criticizes the force of her writing, which Stenton considers antagonized those who would have been reached through moderation. Stenton seems to find distasteful the irregularity of Wollstonecraft's life, and indeed her treatment is a good example of the critic, who, responding with hostility to the life, is therefore hostile to the work, seen as either wrong or inadequate.

A very different attitude toward Wollstonecraft emerges from William Gaunt's book on Blake.[33] In this, Gaunt summarizes Wollstonecraft's life so that she can become the "Romantic Woman," the ideal of the Fuseli-Blake group. He speculates whether Blake might have had Wollstonecraft in mind when writing his poem "Mary," about a woman born "different" and so scorned and envied. Whether or not the inspiration of "Mary," Wollstonecraft is, according to Gaunt, the type of woman toward whom Blake's ideas pointed, "free, passionate, romantic, embracing experience."

Constance Rover discusses Wollstonecraft's life with reference to the lives of other feminist women; through her discussion, she intends to reveal the way in which the feminists were affected by their personal attachments and disappointments.[34] In the section on Wollstonecraft, she suggests that her associations with Godwin and Imlay augmented the connection in the public mind between feminism and immorality.

A study touching on Wollstonecraft's life but not primarily concerned with it is Burton R. Pollin's "Mary Hays on Women's Rights in the *Monthly Magazine.*"[35] This treats Mary Hays, a friend and admirer of Wollstonecraft and, like her, a magazine reviewer. In 1796 she discussed Wollstonecraft's *Letters Written... in Sweden.* In this review she seems to have moved from her initial attitude of unqualified admiration so far as to criticize some phrases of Wollstonecraft, although she does describe her as a writer of considerable eminence. Mary Hays followed Wollstonecraft in arguing for women's rights and after Wollstonecraft's death she wrote an admiring obituary of her friend. Pollin finds reasonable Hays's later omission of Wollstonecraft from *Female Biography,* on the grounds that the biographies were of the illustrious dead of the more distant past. Wardle, however, pointed out in his biography that Wollstonecraft's contemporaries, Catherine Macaulay and Madame Roland, were fully treated and that, although Hays's first obituary was eulogistic, a later biographical sketch was more restrained and apologetic so that the final omission from *Female Biography* would conclude this trend.

BIOGRAPHIES

Wollstonecraft has been well served biographically. The first study by her husband, Godwin, entitled *Memoirs of the Author of "A Vindication of the Rights of Woman,"* is an impressive work, remarkable for its honesty and restraint; it does much to vindicate not only Wollstonecraft but also Godwin himself, who has suffered much from the degenerate image that emerges from the Shelley episode. It is at present available in an Augustus Kelley reprint edition.[36]

The nineteenth- and early twentieth-century biographies of Elizabeth Robins Pennell and Madeline Linford interpret Wollstonecraft more or less adequately for their times.[37] They rely heavily on Godwin and on the work by Kegan Paul. In 1876 Kegan Paul published his biography of Godwin entitled *William Godwin: His Friends and Contemporaries,* in which he treated Wollstonecraft very fully. In 1879, this was followed by a prefatory memoir to an edition of Wollstonecraft's letters to Imlay. In both works, Kegan Paul emphasized Wollstonecraft's unconventionality, but was at pains to extinguish it. He considered her opinions in the main those which most cultivated women held in his time. To support these opinions with the life, he regarded as slander the story of Wollstonecraft's love for Fuseli and his rejection of her. Pennell and Linford elaborate on Kegan Paul's image of Wollstonecraft and they emphasize her virtue and purity of motive.

After the partial success of the feminist movement in 1911, G. R. Stirling Taylor can emphasize, as well as Wollstonecraft's virtue, her passion and fire, qualities he finds in both her life and writings.[38] His book is one of the most sympathetic discussions of Wollstonecraft published in this century. Some years later, in 1928, after the Franchise Act, H. R. James is again enthusiastic concerning Wollstonecraft's power, but significantly for the times he emphasizes her domestic roles, which he finds even more impressive than her public roles of pioneer feminist and author.[39]

With the retrenchment of the feminist movement by 1937, the unexpressed distrust of James toward woman as thinker is expressed in *This Shining Woman: Mary Wollstonecraft Godwin* by George R. Preedy (Mrs. Gabrielle Long).[40] The introduction, pretending to commend the woman if not the author, blames Wollstonecraft for her lack of understanding of the feminine character. Preedy views Wollstonecraft's life as a series of disasters and mistakes, ending in the cool and unfulfilling relationship with William Godwin. Preedy considers Wollstonecraft's fame entirely owing to her situation as a woman, since her works are crude and trite. As a biography of Wollstonecraft, Preedy's book is made worthless by factual errors, but the attitudes the author reveals in it make it significant for the study of Wollstonecraft's posthumous reputation.

By the second half of this century, a new biography of Wollstonecraft was clearly required, one that would counteract the bizarre images created by Preedy and others and one that would interpret Wollstonecraft for her age in the same way as the Pennell and Linford biographies had done for theirs. In addition, there was by 1950 a large quantity of new documents available which would allow a new and scholarly work on Wollstonecraft to be written. In his critical biography, Ralph Wardle draws on this new material, especially that printed by Clark Durant in his Supplement and the Wollstonecraft letters in Lord Abinger's collection.[41]

Wardle relates the facts of Wollstonecraft's life and traces her intellectual growth from conventional to unconventional, using the letters to illustrate the development. In addition, he describes the philosophical and literary tradition of *The Rights of Woman,* as well as eighteenth-century views of women and their education, to which Wollstonecraft is referring, a feature also of Pennell's biography. He presents the reactions to Wollstonecraft's work and briefly traces the later course of the feminist ideas Wollstonecraft helped to promote.

In the course of the biographical account, Wollstonecraft's literary works are assessed. Wardle finds the originality of *The Rights of Woman* in Wollstonecraft's application of her own experience to her general ideas. With Eliot, he sees as the central thesis the idea that the progress of civilization as a whole is deterred when women are deprived of liberty and equality, and he notes Wollstonecraft's analogy between oppressed womankind and oppressed mankind, an analogy that closely connects her two *Vindications.* Wardle considers *The Rights of Men* a failure as a reply to Burke's *Reflections,* although Wollstonecraft is nearest to success when she attacks Burke's assumption that the English government needs no reforming.

The development of the women's movement in the last decade has made some of Wardle's assumptions about women, as well as his assessment of feminist ideas, seem dated. It was because of this and because of Wardle's failure to emphasize Wollstonecraft's situation as a woman that Margaret George wrote her biography entitled *One Woman's "Situation": A Study of Mary Wollstonecraft.*[42] George sees Wollstonecraft's feminism as both a product of her life experience and a response to the revolutionary promises of liberal individualism.

As a work of scholarship, George's book has little to add to Wardle's. It purports to be an interpretation of Wollstonecraft rather than primarily a factual biography. The interpretation is largely a psychological retelling of some of the facts of Wollstonecraft's life with emphasis on certain relationships and events regarded as psychologically significant by the author; for example, Wollstonecraft's alleged identification with her father. The book is marred by shifts in tone from the laudatory to the ironic and the contingent confusion of judgment.[43] In addition, it is frequently condescending to Wollstonecraft and to the concept of woman. In spite of these faults, however, the book is a fairly readable and concise introduction to Wollstonecraft's life.

Another readable and derivative biography published recently is Edna Nixon's *Mary Wollstonecraft: her life and times*.[44] Based mainly on Wardle's biography and edition of the Wollstonecraft-Godwin letters, the work is marked by excessive generalization, rhetorical questions, winking asides about future events, and by rather glaring inaccuracies. Constantly it reveals the idea, common in popular biography, of life as a pattern sketched by an omniscient narrator. One result of this obsession with the full design is the assumption that Wollstonecraft held her mature ideas in her early years.

The last three years have seen three major biographies of Wollstonecraft. The first is Eleanor Flexner's *Mary Wollstonecraft: A Biography*.[45] As smoothly readable as the Nixon and George books, it is, in addition, based on original scholarship. Flexner investigates Wollstonecraft's life, correcting, adding to, or reinterpreting statements by Wardle and earlier biographers. She examines the genesis of Wollstonecraft's thinking and notes the ambiguity of some of her later ideas.

In her introduction, Flexner claims to lay more emphasis on Wollstonecraft's life for the formation of her ideas than on the philosophical movements of the period. This is a useful emphasis, and Flexner's study is valuable in its account of Wollstonecraft's early years, the relationships she entered into, and the emotional roles and stances created from them. Flexner discusses Wollstonecraft's illnesses and quixotic moods, and on modern psychiatric evidence identifies many as repressed anger. This diagnosis should, I think, be given tentatively, as should Flexner's statement that Wollstonecraft saw her father in several of the men who unhappily tangled with her.

In Flexner's book, much emphasis is laid on Wollstonecraft's religion, on her early piety and belief in the value of earthly suffering, stressed earlier in Kegan Paul. Flexner finds the erosion of this belief occurring when suffering seemed to Wollstonecraft unmerited by humanity and unwilled by God.

While stressing Wollstonecraft's religion, Flexner underplays her rationalism, perhaps because she considers the reasoning power that should support it singularly absent from much of Wollstonecraft's work. Flexner makes few critical judgments on this work; yet she suggests her distaste for

xxi

Wollstonecraft's rhetorical and diffuse polemical style in *The Rights of Woman* and for her bitter tone in the letters to Imlay, which Flexner finds "almost too painful to read." She is more sympathetic, however, to the Godwin-Wollstonecraft relationship and the letters expressing it.

In her biography, Flexner differs most clearly from Wardle in her tendency to be critical of Wollstonecraft and skeptical of the picture drawn by Godwin in his *Memoirs*. For example, she finds Wollstonecraft tactless in her dealings with her sisters.

In the second biography of Wollstonecraft, the much publicized *Life and Death of Mary Wollstonecraft,* Claire Tomalin is even more critical of her subject than Flexner.[46] According to the dust cover, the author sees Wollstonecraft as a woman of "imperfect heroism," and the picture she draws confirms this description. Tomalin is especially dubious about Wollstonecraft's part in the removal of her sister, Eliza, from her husband, and she sees as a possible result of this Eliza's rejection of Fanny Imlay many years later. She is also critical of the Wollstonecraft-Godwin marriage, so much admired by Wardle. Tomalin differs from recent biographers in many of her details as well as in her interpretations of several incidents. For example, she and Flexner disagree on the circumstances of Eliza's marriage and delivery. Each bases part of her interpretation of the marriage on the date of the baby's birth; in Flexner's book it follows speedily on the marriage, so suggesting some compulsion in the affair, while in Tomalin's it is much later, so suggesting the marriage as Eliza's choice. The dating then affects each author's attitude toward Wollstonecraft's dramatic abduction.

At the end of Tomalin's book, there is a curious appendix, a review of Mary Hays's *Appeal to the Men of Great Britain in Behalf of Women,* which Tomalin believes unavailable. Far from being so, it has recently been reissued in facsimile by Garland Publishing, Inc.[47]

The Life and Death of Mary Wollstonecraft is an uneven work; illuminating in its discussion of Wollstonecraft's stay in Ireland and of the French feminist movement during the Revolution, it is less so in its treatment of the Price and

Johnson circles, which were so formative of Wollstonecraft's ideas. On the whole, however, the book tells its story well and is in places well researched. It is certainly the wittiest and most fluent of the recent biographies.

Emily Sunstein's *A Different Face,* the final biography, inevitably demands comparison with its immediate predecessors.[48] In original research and scholarship, it cannot measure up to Flexner's book and in urbanity of style it falls short of Tomalin's. It surpasses both, however, in the sympathy and appreciation it reveals for its subject.

The faults of Sunstein's book are more immediately apparent than those of the Flexner and Tomalin works. Often Sunstein substitutes a rather simplistic psychologizing for a careful analysis of Wollstonecraft's character and motives, and she avoids discussing many of the problems of the life, for example Wollstonecraft's literary and emotional relationship with Henry Fuseli. In addition, she makes little attempt to provide Wollstonecraft with a literary and philosophical context, and she fails to treat several problems of scholarship, such as those concerning the genuineness of the Opie portrait and the authorship of the reviews in the *Analytical Review.* Sunstein accepts without dispute Wardle's thesis concerning the extent of these reviews, although Flexner and Derek Roper have thrown considerable doubt over it.

What Sunstein's book lacks in scholarship and breadth of treatment, however, it makes up for in sympathy with its main subject. Unlike Flexner, Sunstein does not seek to avoid the raw pain of Wollstonecraft's life and, unlike Tomalin, she does not inappropriately suggest its irony. She allows Wollstonecraft to appear as a dignified woman, worthy of respect in spite of her many silly actions.

Because of her sympathetic view of Wollstonecraft, Sunstein takes pains to account for certain incidents other biographers have condemned. For example, the abduction of Eliza after her postpartum breakdown is made more understandable in the light of Sunstein's suggestion that Wollstonecraft's brother Henry may have become insane by this time. If this were so— and Sunstein makes a compelling case for it—Wollstonecraft's fears for Eliza's sanity would seem less exaggerated and irrational than they may otherwise do.

Sunstein's book is not of the life-and-works variety, and there is more summary than detailed criticism of Wollstonecraft's book. However, apart from that of *The Wrongs of Woman,* with which Sunstein is clearly out of sympathy, the summaries of the works are just and they attract the reader to the originals.

HISTORICAL AND CRITICAL STUDIES

The first full-length study of Wollstonecraft's works appeared during the feminist movement of the late nineteenth century. Emma Rauschenbusch-Clough treats primarily *A Vindication of the Rights of Woman,* which she relates to works of Godwin and later socialist writers.[49] Clough also provides a survey of the influences on Wollstonecraft's thought, and she shows in what ways she was typical of her age. Clough criticizes her for too closely associating virtue and reason and for ignoring conscience and spontaneous impulses. A final section of the book describes the reception in Germany of Wollstonecraft's ideas.

Two other books discuss Wollstonecraft's works, while placing them in a European context. Jacob Bouten's study, written in 1922, traces the feminist movement from Greek through French and English writers to Wollstonecraft.[50] His book is of most value for its discussion of the French tradition, although it is also useful for its summary of the history and ideas of the English Bluestockings and of their distinction from Wollstonecraft. Hannah More, the most famous of the Bluestockings, wanted partial reform in the position of women, consonant with their divinely appointed subordination, while the French feminists, seeking a measure of emancipation for women, yet felt that their chief aim should be to please. Wollstonecraft, however, wanted a radical change in agreement with her religious opinion, that women like men had immortal souls to create.

A decade later, Marthe Severn Storr again places Wollstonecraft in a European tradition of feminism.[51] She concentrates on Wollstonecraft's religious and ethical ideas, and traces the development and modification of these through the literary works. She provides contrasts and comparisons of Wollstonecraft's ideas with those of other liberal philosophers of the period, such as Rousseau and Godwin. James T. Boulton provides a context for Wollstonecraft's *Vindication of the Rights of Men* in his discussion of political works of the late eighteenth century.[52] He sees Wollstonecraft's opposition to Burke as a humanitarian one; she identifies herself with the poor and regards Burke's inability to do so as a failure of reason. Wollstonecraft sees her attack on Burke as the assault of a rationalist on an imaginative and sentimental writer out of place in a world of politics. Her book is meant as a moral and an intellectual indictment of a man who can respond only to misery when it is royal. The major faults of *The Rights of Men* emerge when Boulton compares it with the *Vindiciae Gallicae,* another answer to Burke. Wollstonecraft's sympathy with Dr. Price and his ideas is too extravagant, and this fact, coupled with her lack of organization, weakens her denunciation of Burke for similar excesses and faults.

Wollstonecraft as a reviewer is the subject of a controversy among Wardle, Derek Roper, and Flexner. In "Mary Wollstonecraft, Analytical Reviewer," Wardle tries to identify the articles Wollstonecraft wrote for the *Analytical Review* during the 1780s and 1790s; on the grounds of subject matter and style, he assigns to her the ones initialled M and W.[53] He assumes that unsigned articles preceding these are also by Wollstonecraft. Through Wollstonecraft's comments on writers, Wardle traces the growth of her radical opinions. In the late 1780s, for example, on the evidence of a review, she seems to approve pedagogical works which assume a certain peculiar irrationality in women; by 1790, however, she is enthusiastic over Catherine Macaulay's radical proposals for the education of women as beings equal in rationality to men.

In response to Wardle, Derek Roper queries the assignment of several articles to Wollstonecraft.[54] He finds fault with the assumption that consecutive reviews by one person have the initial only at the end of the last. Since there are identical signatures on consecutive articles and since consecutive unsigned articles often have extremely varied subjects, he concludes that articles unsigned by Wollstonecraft may not be hers and that those articles far from her signature are unlikely to be hers. In her biography of Wollstonecraft, Flexner goes further, disputing the authorship of some articles allowed to Wollstonecraft by Roper. She suggests, for example, that Fuseli is a more likely author than Wollstonecraft of a review on William Gilpin's *Observations Relative Chiefly to Picturesque Beauty,* which concerns aesthetics. This review was, however, signed W.

Wollstonecraft's novels have attracted little favorable comment. The author is usually regarded as too egotistic to create successful characters, and, when her novels have been studied, it is usually for their autobiographical interest, their record of Wollstonecraft's view of her life, mingled with her desires.

There are two main exceptions to these generalizations. J. M. S. Tompkins discusses Wollstonecraft's two novels in *The Popular Novel in England 1770-1800,* finding *Mary* an example of "a fine theme in inexperienced hands" and seeing in *The Wrongs of Woman* "a novel of propaganda," both "crude" and "deeply interesting."[55] Tompkins' work is primarily useful for the context it provides for Wollstonecraft's novels.

The other exception is a French study which surveys late eighteenth-century female fiction. Philippe Séjourné finds Wollstonecraft's works typical of women's novels in their didactic intention and in their theme of oppressed womanhood.[56] Wollstonecraft's power and originality are revealed in her use of biographical details and in the treatment, in *The Wrongs of Woman,* of subjects regarded as taboo for women writers. The most innovative part of *The Wrongs of Woman* is for Séjourné the recital of the lower class woman, Jemima, whose miseries strike the reader more than the typical literary ones of her bourgeois companion. Séjourné considers that Wollstonecraft's *Rights of Woman* inspired other women authors, such as Mary Hays, to express clearly feminist ideas more directly than they had earlier allowed themselves to do.

The healthy state of Wollstonecraft scholarship is suggested by the growing number of books and articles dealing seriously with her life and work. A full-length critical study of Wollstonecraft's work, by Moira Ferguson and Janet M. Todd, will be appearing shortly, and several articles and dissertations are being written on the life, on particular works, and on the relationship of the works to other literature of the time. In addition, the *Mary Wollstonecraft Newsletter,* which has now been expanded into the journal *Women & Literature,* continues to have Wollstonecraft as a primary interest, and frequently publishes articles on her.

Clearly, the *British Critic* was awry when, in the early 1800s, it predicted a speedy oblivion for Wollstonecraft. Her works and her life are still very much present to us. Undoubtedly she would welcome the intense interest in her work, but perhaps she would be less eager to hear of the arguments over her life. In one of her last letters, she declared herself sick of personal vindications:

> We ought not to be too anxious respecting the opinions of others—I am not fond of vindications . . . as we in general give others credit for worth, in proportion as we possess it—I am easy with regard to the opinions of the *best* part of mankind. I *rest* on my own.[57]

Notes

1. (London: Joseph Johnson, 1792).

2. (London: Joseph Johnson, 1798).

3. *Mary Wollstonecraft: Letters to Imlay* (London: Kegan Paul, 1879); *The Love Letters of Mary Wollstonecraft to Gilbert Imlay* (London: Hutchinson & Co., 1908).

4. (Berkeley: University of California Press, 1937).

5. (Lawrence: University of Kansas Press, 1951); (Lawrence: University of Kansas Press, 1966); (London: Henry S. King, 1876).

6. (London: Constable & Co. Ltd., 1927).

7. (Cambridge: Harvard University Press, 1970). The introductions to the Wollstonecraft material are by Eleanor Flexner and Eleanor Louise Nicholes.

8. (Gainesville: Scholars' Facsimiles & Reprints, 1960).

9. (New York: Norton, 1967); (Harmondsworth: Penguin, 1975).

10. (New York: Harcourt Brace Jovanovich, 1971); New York: Columbia University Press, 1973).

11. *The Feminist Controversy in England 1788-1810* (New York: Garland Publishing, Inc.). *A Vindication of the Rights of Woman* is also included in this series.

12. (Fontwell, Sussex: Centaur Press, 1970).

13. (New York: Scholars' Facsimiles and Reprints, 1975).

14. (New York: Norton, 1975). Oxford University Press is bringing out editions of all Wollstonecraft's novels. The works will have introductions by Gary Kelly.

15. (Gainesville: Scholars' Facsimiles & Reprints, 1964).

16. *Etudes Anglaises* 24, 298-303.

NOTES

17. *Nineteenth Century Fiction,* 17 (June 1962), 78-80.

18. (Gainesville: Scholars' Facsimiles & Reprints, 1962).

19. *Satire Newsletter,* 4 (Fall 1966), 29-34.

20. *Philological Quarterly* (April 1963), 242-248.

21. The work has been reproduced in facsimile by Garland Publishing Inc.

22. *Studies in Burke and His Time,* XVI, 3 (Spring 1975), 271-277.

23. *Modern Woman: The Lost Sex* (1947; Universal Edition, 1959); *Times Literary Supplement* (Sept. 6, 1974), 941-944.

24. Ed. Thomas Pinney (London: Routledge; New York: Columbia University Press, 1963).

25. *An Anthropologist at Work: Writings of Ruth Benedict,* ed. Margaret Mead (Boston: Houghton Mifflin, 1959).

26. (1932; London: Harcourt Edition, 1965).

27. "Mary Wollstonecraft's Residence with Thomas Taylor the Platonist," *Notes and Queries,* IX (1962), 461-463.

28. "An Early Suitor of Mary Wollstonecraft," *PMLA,* 58 (March 1943), 163-169.

29. "Mary Wollstonecraft and William Godwin: A Revolutionary Marriage," *Ms.* (December 1972), 79.

30. (New York: Doubleday & Co., Inc., 1975).

31. (London: Watts, 1957).

32. (London: Allen and Unwin, 1957).

33. *Arrows of Desire: A Study of William Blake and his Romantic World* (London: Museum Press, 1956).

34. *Love, Morals and the Feminists* (London: Routledge & Kegan Paul, 1970).

35. *Etudes Anglaises,* 24, 271-282.

36. (Clifton: Augustus Kelley, 1972).

37. *Life of Mary Wollstonecraft* (London: W. H. Allen, 1885); *Mary Wollstonecraft (1759-1797)* (London: Leonard Parsons, 1924).

38. *Mary Wollstonecraft: A Study in Economics and Romance* (London: Martin Secker, 1911).

39. *Mary Wollstonecraft: A Sketch* (London: Oxford University Press, 1932).

40. (London: Collins, 1937).

41. *Mary Wollstonecraft: A Critical Biography* (Lawrence: University of Kansas Press, 1951).

42. (Urbana: University of Illinois Press, 1970).

43. A similar point was made by Florence Boos in her article "Biographies of Mary Wollstonecraft," *Mary Wollstonecraft Newsletter*, I, 2.

44. (London: Dent, 1971).

45. (New York: Coward, McCann and Geoghegan, 1972).

46. (London: Weidenfeld and Nicolson, 1974).

47. *The Feminist Controversy in England, 1788-1810* (New York: Garland Publishing, Inc.).

48. *A Different Face: The Life of Mary Wollstonecraft* (New York: Harper & Row, 1975).

49. *A Study of Mary Wollstonecraft and the Rights of Woman* (London: Longmans, Green, and Co., 1898).

50. *Mary Wollstonecraft and the Beginning of Female Emancipation in France and England* (Amsterdam: H. J. Paris, 1922).

51. *Mary Wollstonecraft et le Mouvement Féministe dans la Littérature Anglaise* (Paris: Les Presses Universitaires de Paris, 1931).

52. *The Language of Politics in the Age of Wilkes and Burke* (London: Routledge & Kegan Paul, 1963). Wollstonecraft's *Rights of Men* is mentioned again in its political context by R. J. Fennessy in *Burke, Paine and the Rights of Man* (The Hague, 1963). In "A Rhetorical Analysis of Mary Wollstonecraft's *A Vindication of the Rights of Woman*" (Michigan, 1971),

L. K. Hayden evaluates Wollstonecraft's rhetoric in *The Rights of Woman*.

53. *PMLA,* LXII (December 1947), 1000-1009.

54. "Mary Wollstonecraft's Review," *Notes and Queries,* V, 37-38.

55. (1932; Lincoln: University of Nebraska Press, 1961).

56. *Aspects généreaux du roman féminin en Angleterre de 1740 à 1800* (Gap: Louis-Jean, 1966). Other recent studies of the female novel of Wollstonecraft's time include "The Didactic and 'Philosophical' Novel in England, 1792-1805" (Wisconsin, 1964) by W. A. Flanders, which discusses Wollstonecraft's *Wrongs of Woman* among novels showing women victimized by their social position and *Later Women Novelists, 1744-1815* (Cork and Oxford, 1947), by B. G. McCarthy.

57. *Annual Necrology 1797-8* (London: Phillips, 1800).

WORKS

1 Wollstonecraft, Mary. THOUGHTS ON THE EDUCATION OF DAUGHTERS:
WITH REFLECTIONS ON FEMALE CONDUCT, IN THE MORE IMPORTANT DU-
TIES OF LIFE. London: Joseph Johnson, 1787.

The book is a collection of short essays on education and on
the moral and intellectual development of girls. It concerns
teachers, parents, and girls, all of whom are given advice.
The book reveals Wollstonecraft's belief in the supreme importance of environment in the shaping of character. Women are
criticized for their triviality and obsession with ornamenta-
tion, and they are urged to care for their children more seriously.

2 Wollstonecraft, Mary. MARY: A FICTION. London: Joseph Johnson, 1788.

This novel is primarily a fictional presentation of Wollstonecraft's life, whose events it follows closely. The novel concerns an intelligent and sensitive girl, who finds refuge from
an unsympathetic family in a friendship with Ann, clearly a
portrait of Wollstonecraft's friend, Fanny Blood. The heroine's circumstances differ from Wollstonecraft's: she is the
daughter of wealthy parents, who force her to marry the person
of their choice so that two estates will be brought together.
After the marriage, the young husband goes abroad, leaving the
heroine, Mary, to console herself with Ann who, like Fanny
Blood, soon dies. Mary finds later consolation in a love for
Henry, whom she is unable to marry. When Henry dies, Mary re-
turns to her husband and resolves to devote herself to good
works. She looks forward to the next world as a release from
this.

3 Wollstonecraft, Mary. ORIGINAL STORIES FROM REAL LIFE: WITH
CONVERSATIONS CALCULATED TO REGULATE THE AFFECTIONS AND FORM
THE MIND TO TRUTH AND GOODNESS. London: Joseph Johnson,1788.

The preface states that the conversations and tales are accommodated to the present condition of society, which obliges the author to attempt to cure by reason those faults which should never have taken root in the infant mind. The tales are designed to illustrate morals and instruct through example. Mary and Caroline, at the ages of fourteen and twelve, are consigned to the care of Mrs. Mason, who aims to eradicate the prejudices formed in their early years and substitute good habits for those carelessly contracted. There are twenty-five chapters concerning the correct treatment of animals, the benefits arising from beauty of soul, from devotion, and from charity. There are cautionary tales illustrating the effects of anger, lying, indulgence, procrastination, idleness, and affectation. The children are placed in various situations where they may deduce the moral for themselves. For example, in the penultimate chapter, they visit a poor family in London and learn that idleness leads to vice and that generosity requires self-denial and economy.

4   Wollstonecraft, Mary. Translation of Jacques Necker's ON THE
    IMPORTANCE OF RELIGIOUS OPINIONS. London: Joseph Johnson,1788.

In her advertisement, Wollstonecraft states that she has taken some liberties with the text to preserve the spirit of the original.

5   Wollstonecraft, Mary. THE FEMALE READER: OR MISCELLANEOUS
    PIECES, IN PROSE AND VERSE: SELECTED FROM THE BEST WRITERS,
    AND DISPOSED UNDER PROPER HEADS: FOR THE IMPROVEMENT OF YOUNG
    WOMEN. London: Joseph Johnson, 1789.

No copy of this work has been found.

6   Wollstonecraft, Mary. Translation of Madame de Cambon's YOUNG
    GRANDISON. London: Joseph Johnson, 1790.

This is a revision of an earlier translation.

7   Wollstonecraft, Mary. A VINDICATION OF THE RIGHTS OF MEN, IN
    A LETTER TO THE RIGHT HONOURABLE EDMUND BURKE. London: Joseph
    Johnson, 1790.

Wollstonecraft's book is a reply to Edmund Burke's REFLECTIONS ON THE REVOLUTION IN FRANCE. It was inspired by Burke's attack on her friend, Richard Price, and by his irrational reverence for unexamined tradition and for property rights. Wollstonecraft endeavors to prove Burke's inconsistency by comparing statements in the REFLECTIONS with earlier statements in Burke's other works and to prove his insensitivity by calling attention to the evils in England which Burke is said to overlook. Much of A VINDICATION OF THE RIGHTS OF MEN is a direct attack on Burke's character; he is accused of stupidity, crassness, vulgarity, and venality. In addition, he is blamed for his rhetorical descriptions, which obscure his subject matter. Wollstonecraft's book is rambling and digressive and it touches on many subjects, such as aristocratic education, the position

and character of women, and the ridiculous practices of elec-
tioneering.

8   Wollstonecraft, Mary. Translation of Christian Gotthilf Salzmann's ELEMENTS OF MORALITY FOR THE USE OF CHILDREN. London:
Joseph Johnson, 1790-1.

Mary Wollstonecraft states in her advertisement that she began
translating Salzmann's book as an exercise but then found it a
very rational work, whose opinions coincided with her own.
She admits that her translation is not a literal one; she has
made the stories English and has added and altered where neces-
sary. She considers that she has tried to imitate the simplicity of style and manners of the original stories, but has not
copied them. At the end of the advertisement, Wollstonecraft
refers to her own book, ORIGINAL STORIES. . . . which, like
Salzmann's, draws its pictures from real life. The tale about
Indians has, she asserts, been inserted into Salzmann's work
to lead children to consider Indians as their brothers. Ralph
Wardle noted that the story is not so much an insertion as an
alteration of the details of a story by Salzmann (see 677).

9   Wollstonecraft, Mary. A VINDICATION OF THE RIGHTS OF WOMAN
WITH STRICTURES ON POLITICAL AND MORAL SUBJECTS. London: Joseph Johnson, 1792.

The dedication of the work is to Talleyrand in the hope that
it will persuade him to include women in his plan for education
in France. The introduction emphasizes the point that education is Wollstonecraft's main concern. The lack of education
in women is seen as the main source of their misery. Wollstonecraft reveals that her interest is in women of the middle class;
she hopes to persuade them to acquire strength of body and mind
rather than delicacy and weakness, supposedly attractive to men.

The first chapter of A VINDICATION OF THE RIGHTS OF WOMAN makes
general observations about the state of humanity, its habit of
subordination and its need for reason. The second and third
chapters trace the history of misogynist thought with quotations
from such poets as Pope and Milton and such writers as Dr. Gregory. The fourth chapter discusses women's state of degradation
caused by erroneous opinions and faulty education. The fifth
chapter concerns modern writers on women; it is chiefly directed
against Rousseau whose depiction of the ideal woman in Sophie of
EMILE is treated with contempt by Wollstonecraft. The sixth
chapter concerns the false notions of beauty and delicacy taught
to young girls, while the seventh discusses the mistaken idea of
modesty. The eighth chapter treats the pernicious morality of
good reputation and shows how it undermines true morality in
women. Chapter nine takes up points made in chapter one concerning unnatural distinctions in society and the evil effects
they have on both the high and the low. Chapters ten and
eleven concern the relations of children to their parents,
which should, in Wollstonecraft's view, be based on reason
rather than prescription. Chapter twelve outlines a system for

national education for boys and girls. Chapter thirteen describes the various follies Wollstonecraft regards as peculiar
to women. The book ends with the plea for women to share
men's rights so that they can practise their virtues. Throughout the book there are numerous digressions, and most topics
are not confined to one chapter.

10 Wollstonecraft, Mary. AN HISTORICAL AND MORAL VIEW OF THE ORI-
GIN AND PROGRESS OF THE FRENCH REVOLUTION; AND THE EFFECT IT
HAS PRODUCED IN EUROPE. London: Joseph Johnson, 1794.

The book concerns the early period of the French Revolution.
It stops before Wollstonecraft's arrival in France and is not,
therefore, based on any first-hand experience. Nonetheless,
it is informed with knowledge of the later Terror, which occurred during Wollstonecraft's stay in France. Wollstonecraft
tells her story clearly, relying heavily on her sources, especially English periodicals. The view of the French Revolution
that emerges is an evolutionary one. It was the natural consequence of intellectual progress and, in spite of temporary set-
backs, will result in a genuine improvement in France. Her
main fear for France was that it had substituted an aristocracy
of wealth for one of birth, and she is eloquent on the dangers
for a country of excessive commerce and industrialization. The
second half of THE FRENCH REVOLUTION is harsher than the first.
Wollstonecraft is especially severe on the Parisian women who
marched to Versailles and she contrasts them with the true revo-
lutionaries who took the Bastille.

11 Wollstonecraft, Mary. LETTERS WRITTEN DURING A SHORT RESIDENCE
IN SWEDEN, NORWAY, AND DENMARK. London: Joseph Johnson, 1796.

The work is an account of Wollstonecraft's travels through Scandinavia on business for Gilbert Imlay. Although the letters
were designed for publication, there are frequent references in
them to Wollstonecraft's melancholy situation, her past suffer-
ings, and her abandonment by Imlay. There are natural descriptions, accounts of people, manners and customs in each country,
and generalizations from her observations. There are references to her theories of women's education and needs, to her views
on national character and the improvement of nations, and to her
beliefs in the power of environment to determine character.
Constantly Wollstonecraft compares and contrasts the countries
she visits with ones she knows intimately, England and France,
so that she can generalize on the progress of civilization and
the perfectibility of humanity. She is harsh in her judgment
of Sweden; the defects in national character she ascribes to
lack of liberty. The Danes are also criticized for their lack
of refinement and curiosity, again the result of an oppressive
social system. Norway impressed Wollstonecraft more favorably,
and she attributes the Norwegians' greater energy and vitality
to their larger share of liberty. In each country Wollstonecraft praises the areas of wild scenery, but always notes their
drawbacks, especially the lack of complexity and sophistication
in their inhabitants.

12 Wollstonecraft, Mary. POSTHUMOUS WORKS OF THE AUTHOR OF A
VINDICATION OF THE RIGHTS OF WOMAN. London: Joseph Johnson,
1798.

The Wrongs of Woman: or, Maria. A Fragment
According to Wollstonecraft, The Wrongs of Woman was written
to exhibit the misery and oppression peculiar to women that
arise out of the partial laws and customs of society. The
book opens with Maria in an asylum lamenting the loss of her
baby. She has been deposited in this asylum by her husband
who wishes to gain possession of her fortune. Soon after the
opening of the novel, Maria meets Jemima, a representative of
women of the lower class, and Darnford, a character based on
Wollstonecraft's unfaithful American lover, Gilbert Imlay.
Maria and Darnford have in common superior sensibility and
literary tase, and they are quickly attracted to each other.
When Maria escapes from the asylum with the aid of Jemima,
she joins Darnford, who has also made his escape, and they
live together openly; not, however, in perfect happiness for
Maria finds her imagination had pictured a felicity beyond
reality. At this point, the novel breaks off, but a trial
scene, at which Maria describes the many evils inherent in
women's social situation, was partially completed and was to
have been the climax of the novel. Notes for the conclusion
suggest that Darnford was to prove unfaithful and that Maria
was to attempt suicide. In one note she is successful; in
another she is saved by Jemima and persuaded to live for her
child. The main portion of the book as it stands consists of
narrative accounts of the past lives of the three main characters, Maria, Jemima, and Darnford. Between them, Jemima and
Maria suffer most of the miseries possible to women in the
middle and lower classes. Other minor characters in their
narratives complete the picture with accounts of their own
wrongs. Thus, Wollstonecraft can claim in her preface that
the novel is not the history of an individual but of woman.

Letters
A series of seventy-eight letters written by Wollstonecraft
to Gilbert Imlay, her American lover, are edited and printed
here by William Godwin. They record the relationship of
Wollstonecraft and Imlay, the growing affection of Wollstonecraft for her child, Fanny Imlay, and the gradual realization
of Imlay's desertion. The letters are written from France,
England, and Scandinavia.

Letter on the Present Character of the French Nation.
This letter, intended as an introduction to "a Series of Letters," is the only one completed. It reflects the disillusion
with France which Wollstonecraft felt shortly after her arrival. Amazed by the frivolity and superficiality of the French,
as well as by their recent cruelties, she cannot find the liberty she once expected, and she considers that names only and
not principles have been changed. Wollstonecraft's understanding of the situation in France severely shakes her belief in
the perfectibility of humanity.

Fragment of Letters on the Management of Infants

The fragment reveals that, in the completed work, Wollstonecraft would have aimed to "shew what modes appear to me necessary, to render the infancy of children more healthy and
happy." She considers that the major fault in child raising
is a deviation from simplicity, and she believes the fault
can be cured by an exercise of reason on the part of mothers.

Letters to Mr. Johnson, Bookseller, in St. Paul's Church-Yard.
This section consists of sixteen letters, most of them written
to Joseph Johnson between 1787 and 1792. The early ones speak
much of Wollstonecraft's melancholy moods and illnesses. The
final one is a description written in France of the French
King's procession through the streets of Paris to his trial.
The letters include two sharp notes from Wollstonecraft re-
jecting a man who had proposed a mercenary marriage to her.

Extract of the Cave of Fancy. A Tale.
This is a moral tale about a sage who, finding an orphaned girl
on the sea shore, resolves to raise her according to his own
educational principles. He conjures up a spirit to instruct
the child with the tale of her earthly life. This tale turns
out to be the usual Wollstonecraftian one of a young girl, en-
dowed with much sensibility, who marries against her inclina-
tion. The circumstances of the young girl's life resemble
those of Wollstonecraft's life: there is a profligate father
and a passive mother who relies on her daughter for assistance.

On Poetry, and Our Relish for the Beauties of Nature.
The essay endeavours to answer the question why the beauties
of nature are not really appreciated by most people although
they pretend to appreciate them. Wollstonecraft concludes
that many people are more interested in a scene described by
a poet than in a view of nature. With some differences, this
essay was first printed as a letter signed "W. Q." in the
Monthly Magazine, 1797.

Hints
These are discrete paragraphs primarily concerning women, education, and virtue.

13   [Wollstonecraft, Mary.]   THE EMIGRANTS.   London: A. Hamilton,
     1793.

     In his introduction to the 1964 Scholars' Facsimiles and Re-
     prints edition, Robert R. Hare makes a case for Wollstonecraft's
     authorship of this book, usually ascribed to Gilbert Imlay (see
     also 473).

Wollstonecraft contributed reviews to THE ANALYTICAL REVIEW from
the summer of 1788 to the summer of 1792, when she left for France,
and from the summer of 1796 until her death in 1797. Since the reviews in THE ANALYTICAL REVIEW are unsigned, in most cases it is
impossible to state with certainty whether or not Wollstonecraft
is the author of a particular review. The review of Catherine Macaulay's LETTERS ON EDUCATION has been ascribed to Wollstonecraft
and concerns material later used in A VINDICATION OF THE RIGHTS OF

WOMAN. Because of its interest, it has been included here.

14 [Wollstonecraft, Mary.] ANALYTICAL REVIEW, VIII, September -
December 1790, 241-254.

In her review of Catherine Macaulay's LETTERS ON EDUCATION:
WITH OBSERVATIONS ON RELIGIOUS AND METAPHYSICAL SUBJECTS,
Wollstonecraft summarizes the book and reveals her agreement
with most of the arguments. Much of the review consists of
quotation from Macaulay's work. Wollstonecraft finds Macaulay a masculine and fervid writer and she considers that her
book displays a store of knowledge, arranged by a sound understanding. She especially agrees with Macaulay's views on the
value of home education and on the need to educate boys and
girls in the same way. She also praises Macaulay for her understanding that education should be appropriate to the age
and level of the child. Wollstonecraft believes, however,
that children should be allowed to indulge imagination a little more than Macaulay allows. Wollstonecraft closes her review with praise of Macaulay as a woman writer and moralist.

15 ABERDEEN MAGAZINE: OR, UNIVERSAL REPOSITORY, III, August 1798, 365 - 368.

The review of Godwin's MEMOIRS is favorable to the work and its subject. Wollstonecraft's views on marriage are discussed. Her liaisons are justified because of her fidelity in love. The review continues in III, September 1798, 417-420, with a description of her relationship with Godwin. The facts of Wollstonecraft's life are taken from Godwin's MEMOIRS.

16 ALLGEMEINE LITERATUR-ZEITUNG VOM JAHRE 1798.

There are several references to Wollstonecraft and her fame.

17 ANALYTICAL REVIEW, OR HISTORY OF LITERATURE, DOMESTIC AND FOREIGN, III, January - April 1789, 41-48.

The review of Wollstonecraft's translation of Necker's ON THE IMPORTANCE OF RELIGIOUS OPINIONS is probably by Wollstonecraft herself. The review summarizes the argument of Necker's book, stressing the idea that religion is necessary to morality and a belief in immortality necessary to virtue. The book is seen as revealing a lively imagination and a sure reason, but the style is considered labored. The epithets used for God are not appropriate and are repeated too often. The lack of organization in the book is especially censured, and the whole is said to be unequally written, with eloquent and turgid passages intermixed. The faults in style, in the reviewer's opinion, justify some liberties taken by the translator.

18 ANALYTICAL REVIEW, OR HISTORY OF LITERATURE, DOMESTIC AND FOREIGN, VIII, September - December 1790, 416-419.

The review of Wollstonecraft's VINDICATION OF THE RIGHTS OF MEN mocks Burke's chivalrous attitude toward "the fair sex" and surmises his annoyance at finding his adversary a woman. The arguments of THE RIGHTS OF MEN are summarized, and reference is made to Wollstonecraft's many agreeable digressions. The reviewer judges the sentiments to be just and the language elegant. Doubt is, however, thrown on Wollstonecraft's assertion that Burke was receiving a large pension from Ireland.

19 ANALYTICAL REVIEW, OR HISTORY OF LITERATURE, DOMESTIC AND FOREIGN, IX, January - April 1791, 101.

The review of Salzmann's ELEMENTS OF MORALITY FOR THE USE OF CHILDREN mentions that the book was translated by Wollstonecraft. There is a quotation from her advertisement, in which she states that the translation is not a servile or even a literal one. The review is continued in XI, August - December 1791, 217-220.

20 ANALYTICAL REVIEW, OR HISTORY OF LITERATURE, DOMESTIC AND
    FOREIGN, XII, January – April 1792, 241-249.

    The review of Wollstonecraft's VINDICATION OF THE RIGHTS OF
    WOMAN gives a chapter by chapter summary of its arguments and
    quotes liberally from the work. Wollstonecraft is praised
    for her recognition that men have made sexual objects of
    women and for her courage in expressing her ideas. The re-
    view concludes by describing THE RIGHTS OF WOMAN as a trea-
    tise of female education, which, if its precepts were followed,
    would make the nation better, wiser and happier.

    The review is continued in XIII, May – August 1792, 481-489.
    This section of the review primarily concerns Wollstonecraft's
    strictures on other writers on women, such as Rousseau, Dr.
    Gregory, and Mrs. Piozzi, as well as her proposals for the
    education of women. The book is recommended to all classes of
    society.

21 ANALYTICAL REVIEW, OR HISTORY OF LITERATURE, DOMESTIC AND
    FOREIGN, XX, September – December 1794, 337-347.

    The reviewer of Wollstonecraft's HISTORICAL AND MORAL VIEW OF
    THE ORIGIN AND PROGRESS OF THE FRENCH REVOLUTION describes the
    book as a serious work. It is praised for its energy of dic-
    tion, for its richness of imagery, and especially for its im-
    partiality and solidity of thought. The work is summarized,
    and many long excerpts from it are given.

    The review is concluded in XXI, January – June 1795, 8-17.
    Wollstonecraft's book is here described as a work of uncommon
    merit, containing a great variety of just and important ob-
    servations on the recent affairs in France.

22 ANALYTICAL REVIEW, OR HISTORY OF LITERATURE, DOMESTIC AND
    FOREIGN, XXI, January – June 1795, 396-397.

    This review of John Henry Colls's POETICAL EPISTLE ADDRESSED
    TO MISS WOLLSTONECRAFT (see 38) criticizes Colls for his lack
    of understanding of Wollstonecraft's book on the French Revo-
    lution. The poem is described as rather a compliment to the
    sex than to Wollstonecraft herself. The author is said to
    have adopted in a superficial way the doctrines of A VINDICA-
    TION OF THE RIGHTS OF WOMAN.

23 ANALYTICAL REVIEW, OR HISTORY OF LITERATURE, DOMESTIC AND
    FOREIGN, XXIII, January – June 1796, 229.

    The reviewer of LETTERS WRITTEN DURING A SHORT RESIDENCE IN
    SWEDEN, NORWAY, AND DENMARK praises Wollstonecraft as an in-
    genious writer whose talents are far above the ordinary level.
    In this book she excells as a writer of travels, as formerly
    she had excelled as a writer of educational and philosophical
    works. The LETTERS WRITTEN. . . IN SWEDEN are described as
    spontaneous and the descriptions of nature are regarded
    as sketches rather than finished paintings. The reviewer

states that the work reveals that Wollstonecraft has suffered deeply from a recent affliction.

24 ANALYTICAL REVIEW, OR HISTORY OF LITERATURE, DOMESTIC AND FOREIGN, XXVII, January - June 1798, 235-240.

This review of Godwin's MEMOIRS gives limited praise to the work and its subject, Wollstonecraft. THE MEMOIRS is said to be deficient in its history of the formation of Wollstonecraft's mind. The reviewer notes Wollstonecraft's irregularities of conduct, but also notes her constancy and depth of feeling.

25 ANALYTICAL REVIEW, OR HISTORY OF LITERATURE, DOMESTIC AND FOREIGN, XXVII, January - June 1798, 240-245.

This review of Wollstonecraft's POSTHUMOUS WORKS praises THE WRONGS OF WOMAN, although it finds some fault with its style. The LETTERS TO IMLAY are singled out for special commendation.

26 ANTI-JACOBIN REVIEW AND MAGAZINE: OR, MONTHLY POLITICAL AND LITERARY CENSOR, I, 1798, 91-93.

In a review of MARIA, OR THE WRONGS OF WOMAN by Wollstonecraft, the novel is described as a tale intended to illustrate the doctrines of A VINDICATION OF THE RIGHTS OF WOMAN. The review considers Wollstonecraft failed in her attempt to prove that her heroine's misfortunes arose from the unequal state of women in society; in fact they arose from her injudicious choice of a husband. There is a hostile summary of the book.

27 ANTI-JACOBIN REVIEW AND MAGAZINE: OR, MONTHLY POLITICAL AND LITERARY CENSOR, I, 1798, 94-102.

In a review of Godwin's MEMOIRS, it is stated that Wollstonecraft's life, as it is presented in the MEMOIRS, is not an example to others but a warning. Wollstonecraft's literary works are attacked; A VINDICATION OF THE RIGHTS OF MEN is described as extravagant and trite and A VINDICATION OF THE RIGHTS OF WOMAN as superficial and derivative. The review sees Wollstonecraft as an illustration of Jacobin immorality. It blames her immorality on her defective education when young. There is an attack on the ANALYTICAL REVIEW for its sympathetic account of Wollstonecraft's history and works.

28 ANTI-JACOBIN REVIEW AND MAGAZINE: OR, MONTHLY POLITICAL AND LITERARY CENSOR, I, 1798, 668.

In a review of a novel entitled GERALDINA, it is stated that the doctrines put forward in it are those of Wollstonecraft as they are illustrated in her WRONGS OF WOMAN.

29 ANTI-JACOBIN REVIEW AND MAGAZINE: OR, MONTHLY POLITICAL AND LITERARY CENSOR, II, 1799, 327-329.

In a section concerning the ANALYTICAL REVIEW, Wollstonecraft is mentioned as Godwin's wife.

30 ANTI-JACOBIN REVIEW AND MAGAZINE: OR, MONTHLY POLITICAL AND
    LITERARY CENSOR, III, May 1799, 27-33.

    A footnote to a review of R. Polwhele's UNSEX'D FEMALES sum-
    marizes Godwin's sketch of Wollstonecraft's life in his MEM-
    OIRS. Much is made of her lack of religion when close to
    death.

31. Bage, Robert. HERMSPRONG; OR MAN AS HE IS NOT. London:
    1796. (Turnstile Press, 1951).

    Robert Bage alludes to Wollstonecraft's feminist theories.
    He declares that, while women think so much of their charms,
    Wollstonecraft must write in vain.

32 BRITISH CRITIC, A NEW REVIEW, VI, 1795, 29-36.

    The reviewer of AN HISTORICAL AND MORAL VIEW OF THE ORIGIN AND
    PROGRESS OF THE FRENCH REVOLUTION accuses Wollstonecraft of
    taking her facts and opinions from the NEW ANNUAL REGISTER.
    The accusation is supported by a detailed comparison of several
    of Wollstonecraft's passages with those appearing in the REGIS-
    TER. Wollstonecraft's political and moral ideas are also crit-
    icized as well as her stylistic habits. The volume is said to
    contain much trite declamation.

33 BRITISH CRITIC, A NEW REVIEW, VII, 1796, 602-610.

    This is on the whole a favorable review of Wollstonecraft's
    LETTERS WRITTEN. . . IN SWEDEN. Wollstonecraft is judged to
    have been improved by her experiences of marriage and mother-
    hood. However, the review criticizes her liberal opinions.

34 BRITISH CRITIC, A NEW REVIEW, XII, 1798, 228-233.

    The reviewer of Godwin's MEMOIRS finds distasteful Godwin's
    detailed description of his wife's death, as well as his state-
    ments of her final atheism. The reviewer is most struck by
    Godwin's descriptions of Wollstonecraft's poor relationship
    with her father and of her irregular relationships with Fuseli
    and Imlay. The reviewer ends with a discussion of Wollstone-
    craft's religion, expressing surprise at the discrepancy be-
    tween her opinions in A VINDICATION OF THE RIGHTS OF WOMAN and
    her opinions at the time of her death, as they are described
    by Godwin.

35 BRITISH CRITIC, A NEW REVIEW, XII, 1798, 234-235.

    In this review of Wollstonecraft's POSTHUMOUS WORKS, there is
    a hostile summary of THE WRONGS OF WOMAN. The system of mor-
    ality displayed in the work is said to be offensive to the
    purity of female virtue, and the precepts of religion. Woll-
    stonecraft is described as a woman of strong intellect and un-
    governable passions. She was a sensualist without refinement.
    The other works in POSTHUMOUS WORKS are briefly mentioned.

36   BRITISH CRITIC, A NEW REVIEW, XIV, 1799, 70-71.

In a review of THE UNSEX'D FEMALES, only the speech provided
for Wollstonecraft is commended. It is quoted at length.

37   BRITISH CRITIC, A NEW REVIEW, XXI, 1803, 690-691.

The review of A DEFENCE OF THE CHARACTER AND CONDUCT OF THE
LATE MARY WOLLSTONECRAFT GODWIN describes Wollstonecraft as
already almost forgotten by the public at large. It refers
to admissions about Wollstonecraft's conduct which render
the excessive praise in A DEFENCE ludicrous. Wollstonecraft
is regarded as eccentric, presumptuous, and self-conceited in
her views and ungovernable in her passions.

38   Colls, John Henry. A POETICAL EPISTLE ADDRESSED TO MISS
WOLLSTONECRAFT, OCCASIONED BY READING HER CELEBRATED ESSAY
ON THE RIGHTS OF WOMAN, AND HER HISTORICAL AND MORAL VIEW
OF THE FRENCH REVOLUTION. London: Vernon & Hood, 1795.

John Henry Colls expresses in poetry some of the sentiments
of Wollstonecraft in A VINDICATION OF THE RIGHTS OF WOMAN.

39   Cooper, Thomas. A REPLY TO MR. BURKE'S INVECTIVE. London:
Joseph Johnson, 1792.

Reference is made to Wollstonecraft's VINDICATION OF THE RIGHTS
OF WOMAN and its attack on male despotism.

40   CRITICAL REVIEW, OR ANNALS OF LITERATURE, LXX, 1790, 694-696.

The reviewer of Wollstonecraft's VINDICATION OF THE RIGHTS OF
MEN is hostile to the book and apologizes for having to address
a woman so bluntly.

41   CRITICAL REVIEW, OR ANNALS OF LITERATURE, 1792, 359-398;
1792, 132-141.

The reviewer quotes lavishly from A VINDICATION OF THE RIGHTS
OF WOMAN and tries to show that Wollstonecraft's reasoning must
be wrong since her conclusions are palpably so. The indelicacy
of ideas and expression is especially criticized, and Wollstonecraft is advised to obtain delicacy, elegance, and sensibility
so that she will become pleasing and so achieve happiness. The
reviewer objects to the language of THE RIGHTS OF WOMAN; it is
described as flowery and flowing, as well as weak, diffuse, and
confused.

42   CRITICAL REVIEW, OR ANNALS OF LITERATURE, XVI, 1796, 209-212.

In a review of LETTERS WRITTEN DURING A SHORT RESIDENCE IN
SWEDEN, NORWAY, AND DENMARK, Wollstonecraft is described as an
ingenious writer, but one not always correct in her sentiments
and style. The book under review is considered interesting
but insufficiently organized.

43 CRITICAL REVIEW: OR ANNALS OF LITERATURE,XVI, 1796, 390-396.

The review of AN HISTORICAL AND MORAL VIEW OF THE ORIGIN AND
PROGRESS OF THE FRENCH REVOLUTION considers the book a criti-
que of the French Revolution rather than a history. The review notes Wollstonecraft's just remarks and forcible observations, as well as her want of grace and turgidity. She is
advised in the future volumes of the work to confine herself
either to clear narrative without digressions or to reflections without narrative.

44 CRITICAL REVIEW: OR ANNALS OF LITERATURE, New Arrangement,
XXII, 1798, 414-419.

In this review of Godwin's MEMOIRS and Wollstonecraft's POST-
HUMOUS WORKS, Wollstonecraft is praised for having genius,
although her principles are decried as contrary to well being.
The reviewer finds distasteful her irregular relationships,
which may serve as a warning to others against transgressing
moral codes. In the discussion of POSTHUMOUS WORKS, the reviewer concentrates primarily on THE WRONGS OF WOMAN whose
style and vigor are praised but whose moral tendencies are
condemned. THE LETTERS TO IMLAY and smaller pieces are
briefly praised.

45 Dyer, George. POEMS. London: J. Johnson, 1792.

In his ode "On Liberty," George Dyer mentions Wollstonecraft
as a defender of liberty. A footnote records Dyer's observation that the most sensible women are more uniformly on the
side of liberty than the other sex.

46 EUROPEAN MAGAZINE, AND LONDON REVIEW, XV, 1789, 28-31.

This is a review of Wollstonecraft's translation of Necker's
OF THE IMPORTANCE OF RELIGIOUS OPINIONS. The translation is
described as just and spirited, but with the appearance of
having been hastily executed. The reviewer advises that the
work be carefully revised if a second edition is required.
The review continues on pp. 210-213.

47 EUROPEAN MAGAZINE, AND LONDON REVIEW, XXXIII, 1798, 246-252.

The review of Godwin's MEMOIRS is extremely hostile both to
Wollstonecraft and to her feminist ideas. She is described
as an unhappy woman whose frailties should have been buried
in oblivion. There is a long summary of the events of Wollstonecraft's life. It is regarded as a warning against de-
fying social laws. The review tries to implicate Wollstonecraft in the scandal concerning her former pupil, Mary King.
It ends with the statement that Godwin's book will be read
with disgust by every female who has any pretensions to delicacy and with detestation by everyone attached to religion
and morality.

48 GENERAL MAGAZINE AND IMPARTIAL REVIEW, VI, 1792, 187-191.

The review of A VINDICATION OF THE RIGHTS OF WOMAN is, in general, favorable in its comments.

49 GENTLEMAN'S MAGAZINE; FOR JANUARY, 1791, LXI, 151-4.

The review of A VINDICATION OF THE RIGHTS OF MEN ridicules the idea of the rights of men being asserted by a woman. It discusses Wollstonecraft's attack on property which it sees as against Scripture. Wollstonecraft's optimistic belief in education and perfectibility is especially scorned. Although her rhapsodical bombast is deplored, the reviewer considers that Wollstonecraft has a few strong expressions.

50 GENTLEMAN'S MAGAZINE: AND HISTORICAL CHRONICLE FOR THE YEAR 1797, LXVII, 894.

The obituary praises Wollstonecraft's intellectual gifts and her character. It summarizes her literary career. It ends by stating that the tribute is paid in spite of the author's dislike of the system Wollstonecraft supported in her writings and in her life.

51 GENTLEMAN'S MAGAZINE: AND HISTORICAL CHRONICLE FOR THE YEAR 1798, LXVIII, 186-187.
A letter concerns Godwin's MEMOIRS.
It considers that delicacy should have prompted concealment of certain circumstances of Wollstonecraft's life, especially the affair with Imlay, the suicide attempts, and Wollstonecraft's insensibility during her last illness. Her miserable death is contrasted with the serene and Christian deaths of Addison and Lyttelton.

52 Godwin, William. MEMOIRS OF THE AUTHOR OF A VINDICATION OF THE RIGHTS OF WOMAN. London: Joseph Johnson, 1798.

William Godwin, Wollstonecraft's husband, declares that he is writing the MEMOIRS to prevent malignant representation of the facts of his wife's life. Godwin sketches the main incidents of Wollstonecraft's life, giving short accounts of her various literary works. He describes, although not in great detail, the irregular liaisons into which she entered before her marriage. He is more detailed in his account of his relationship with her. Throughout the book there are testimonies of Godwin's affection for Wollstonecraft and his appreciation of her character.

53 GOTTINGISCHE ANZEIGEN VON GELAHRTEN SACHEN III, 1799, 1520.

This review of Godwin's MEMOIRS praises the work for its warmth and vividness. It criticizes Wollstonecraft's life, which should not be taken as a model. (See Pollin 513).

54 Hamilton,Elizabeth. TRANSLATION OF THE LETTERS OF A HINDOO RAJAH. London: G. G. and J. Robinson, 1796.

Miss Ardent appears to be a picture of Wollstonecraft.

55 Hays, Mary. Preface to LETTERS AND ESSAYS, MORAL AND MISCELL-
    ANEOUS. London: Thomas Knott, 1793.

    In her Preface, Mary Hays quotes from Wollstonecraft's VINDI-
    CATION OF THE RIGHTS OF WOMAN. She pays tribute to the virtue
    and talents of Wollstonecraft.

56 Hays, Mary. "Mary Wollstonecraft," ANNUAL NECROLOGY 1797-1798.
    London: Phillips, 1800.

    Mary Hays gives a lengthy account of Wollstonecraft's life.
    She justifies her actions and explains her philosophy. In
    passing, she refers to the campaign of malice and slander to
    which Wollstonecraft and other radical women have been sub-
    jected. Hays relates Wollstonecraft to previous women writers,
    especially Catherine Macaulay. Many of the facts of Wollstone-
    crafts's life derive from Godwin's MEMOIRS.

57 THE HISTORICAL, BIOGRAPHICAL, LITERARY AND SCIENTIFIC MAGAZINE,
    I, 1799, 27-34.

    This review of Godwin's MEMOIRS calls it the most hurtful book
    of 1798. The book is described as Godwin's history of the
    amours and licence of his wife. It makes Wollstonecraft into
    a warning rather than a model for other women. The reviewer
    is amazed at Godwin's candor concerning Wollstonecraft's af-
    fairs with Fuseli and Imlay, her suicide attempt, and her ir-
    regular relationship with the author. He especially condemns
    her atheism, exemplified in her death.

58 THE HISTORICAL, BIOGRAPHICAL, LITERARY AND SCIENTIFIC MAGAZINE,
    I, 1799, 118.

    A footnote mentions Wollstonecraft.

59 LADY'S MONTHLY MUSEUM OR POLITE REPOSITORY OF AMUSEMENT AND
    INSTRUCTION, III, 1799, 433.

    A letter, supposed to be from a mother, bewails the influence
    on the children of Wollstonecraft's VINDICATION OF THE RIGHTS
    OF WOMAN. The writer relates the effect of this dreadful work
    on each of her daughters. One takes up hunting; one becomes a
    disciple of ancient philosophy; one studies anatomy; and the
    last has begun swearing.

60 LITERARY MAGAZINE AND BRITISH REVIEW FOR 1792, VIII, 133-139.

    The review of Wollstonecraft's VINDICATION OF THE RIGHTS OF
    WOMAN quotes liberally from the work, which is said to contain
    many solid and entertaining reflections. Especially commended
    are Wollstonecraft's reflections on the army. The main writers
    whom Wollstonecraft attacks are briefly discussed.

61 MAGASIN ENCYCLOPEDIQUE OU JOURNAL DES SCIENCES DES LETTRES ET
    DES ARTS, IV, 1798, 555.

There is a short obituary of Wollstonecraft, with mention of her death in childbirth.

62 MAGASIN ENCYCLOPEDIQUE, OU JOURNAL DES SCIENCES, DES LETTRES ET DES ARTS, VI, 1798, 482-493.

A review of Godwin's MEMOIRS of Wollstonecraft is hostile to the book, which is described as shocking and revolting. Wollstonecraft's conduct with Godwin and Imlay is described, and the contrast between her theory in her educational books and her practice is pointed out. Lengthy quotations invite the reader's condemnation of the book.

63 Mathias, T. J. THE SHADE OF ALEXANDER POPE ON THE BANKS OF THE THAMES. AT TWITNAM. A SATIRE; WITH NOTES. London: T. Becket, 1799.

T. J. Mathias attacks both Wollstonecraft and Godwin. Wollstonecraft is portrayed as passion's slave. Her works and Godwin's MEMOIRS are seen as handbooks of debauchery.

64 MONTHLY MAGAZINE AND AMERICAN REVIEW, I, no. 1, 1799, 330-335.

In a section entitled "Reflections on the Character of Mary Wollstonecraft Godwin," the reviewer begins with fulsome praise of Wollstonecraft, seen as one of the truly great characters of the world. To the reviewer she was a being raised above common life. Her last works and Godwin's MEMOIRS, however, reveal her to have deviated far from the pure and revolutionary image; instead she was a prey of ungovernable sensibility. The reviewer harshly condemns her suicide attempts. Her purity of heart is never in question but her acts deserve much blame.

65 THE MONTHLY MAGAZINE AND BRITISH REGISTER FOR 1796, I, February - June 1796, 278-281.

The article by "Christiana," probably Mary Hays, concerns Wollstonecraft's LETTERS WRITTEN. . . IN SWEDEN. The work is praised for its acuteness of observation and its poignancy of feeling, but condemned for its occasional inaccuracy of expression.

66 THE MONTHLY MAGAZINE AND BRITISH REGISTER FOR 1797, III, January - June 1797, 279-282.

A letter signed "W.Q." is by Wollstonecraft. With some changes, it was reprinted in POSTHUMOUS WORKS as the essay "On Poetry, and our Relish for the Beauties of Nature."

67 THE MONTHLY MAGAZINE AND BRITISH REGISTER, IV, September 1797, 232-233.

The obituary notice by Mary Hays praises Wollstonecraft effusively, mentioning her great talents and understanding, her qualities of heart and her powers of indignation. Wollstonecraft is presented as an active fighter for women. Her life is seen as sorrowful and hard; she was a victim of the vices and prejudices of mankind. Finally she achieved happiness only to have it snatched from her. Hays testifies to the power of inspiration Wollstonecraft exerted for many women.

68 THE MONTHLY MAGAZINE AND BRITISH REGISTER, IV, October 1797, 245.

A letter from Mary Hays states that she wrote the obituary of Wollstonecraft printed in the MONTHLY MAGAZINE for September 1797. She expresses pride in her friendship with Wollstonecraft, and she refers to the biography soon to be published by Godwin.

69 THE MONTHLY MAGAZINE AND BRITISH REGISTER, V, May 1798, 355.

A letter refers to the MEMOIRS of Wollstonecraft and concerns Godwin's views on public prayers.

70 THE MONTHLY MAGAZINE AND BRITISH REGISTER, V, July 1798, 493.

A review of Godwin's MEMOIRS describes the work as meagre and rather simple. Wollstonecraft's character is briefly discussed; mention is made of her virtues, as well as her many faults. The POSTHUMOUS WORKS are named but not discussed.

71 THE MONTHLY MAGAZINE AND BRITISH REGISTER, VII, July 1799, 542-543.

In an account of recent literature, there is mention of the vicious attacks on Wollstonecraft in George Walker's THE VAGABOND (see 123).

72 THE MONTHLY MIRROR: REFLECTING MEN AND MANNERS, I, 1795-6, 131-133.

A section entitled "Mrs. Wollstonecraft" describes the author's attempt to write a biographical sketch of Wollstonecraft. The request to Joseph Johnson for information was refused, and the author emphasizes the rudeness of the refusal. The section ends with a statement of how the journal had intended to compliment Wollstonecraft on the strength and vigor of her intellect and the bold delivery of her sentiments.

73 THE MONTHLY MIRROR: REFLECTING MEN AND MANNERS, I, 1795-6, 285-289.

Wollstonecraft's LETTERS WRITTEN DURING A SHORT RESIDENCE IN SWEDEN, NORWAY, AND DENMARK is judged similar to other books of travels. Wollstonecraft is described as a political traveller ready to find fault with the laws and government of three countries she barely knows. The book is found to be unoriginal and full of cant. It is, in addition, blamed for its inconsistency of sentiment and its confusion of expression.

74 THE MONTHLY MIRROR: REFLECTING MEN AND MANNERS, V, 1798,
153-157.

The review concerns both Godwin's MEMOIRS and Wollstonecraft's
POSTHUMOUS WORKS. It gives a balanced assessment of both
works. It finds little interesting in the MEMOIRS and it criticizes the repetition in the work. It is especially critical
of Godwin's minute descriptions of his wife's death. THE
WRONGS OF WOMAN is referred to as a mutilated work; the miseries of the characters are too great and the style is freqently
inflated. The description of Maria is, however, praised. The
review commends the LETTERS TO IMLAY.

75 THE MONTHLY REVIEW; OR, LITERARY JOURNAL, LXXVIII, January -
June 1788, 258.

The review of Wollstonecraft's THOUGHTS ON THE EDUCATION OF
DAUGHTERS praises the book for its sensible remarks on the
instruction of girls. The style is described as correct and
agreeable, and the observations are considered judicious.
The reviewer notes Wollstonecraft's dislike of the novel as
one cause of the affectation in young women.

76 THE MONTHLY REVIEW; OR, LITERARY JOURNAL, IV, January - April
1791, 95-97.

The review of A VINDICATION OF THE RIGHTS OF MEN blames Wollstonecraft for mixing her ideas so as to perplex the reader
and herself. Her style is criticized. Yet the reviewer
praises the many judicious remarks in the work and comments
on Wollstonecraft's love of liberty, humanity, and virtue.

77 THE MONTHLY REVIEW; OR, LITERARY JOURNAL, VII, January - April
1792, 114.

This is a short, favorable review of Salzmann's ELEMENTS OF
MORALITY translated by Wollstonecraft.

78 THE MONTHLY REVIEW; OR, LITERARY JOURNAL,VIII, May - August
1792, 198-209.

This lengthy review of Wollstonecraft's VINDICATION OF THE
RIGHTS OF WOMAN begins with a statement concerning the intellectual improvement in contemporary women. It defines
Wollstonecraft's aim as the correction of errors in female
character and the elevation of women from a state of degradation and vassalage to their proper place in the scale
of existence. The review quotes liberally from A VINDICA-
TION OF THE RIGHTS OF WOMAN and commends many of its sections, for example those contrasting fashionable and rational women, and the qualities of modesty and humility.
Wollstonecraft is judged to be a woman of great energy of
intellect and vigor of fancy. Some of her opinions are,
however, considered fanciful and her projects romantic, especially that concerning women's participation in civil government.

79   THE MONTHLY REVIEW; OR, LITERARY JOURNAL, XVI, January -
      APRIL 1795, 393-402.

      The reviewer considers Wollstonecraft's HISTORICAL AND MORAL
      VIEW OF THE ORIGIN AND PROGRESS OF THE FRENCH REVOLUTION an
      account of the significance of the Revolution rather than
      primarily a record of facts. Wollstonecraft is considered
      well qualified for the work because of her vigorous mind.
      She is praised for not commending indiscriminately all of
      the proceedings in revolutionary France. The main passages
      quoted are those which deal with the causes of the Revolu-
      tion and the taking of the Bastille. On the whole, Woll-
      stonecraft's style is praised, although some imperfections
      in it are noted.

80   THE MONTHLY REVIEW; OR, LITERARY JOURNAL, XX, May - August
      1796, 251-257.

      The reviewer of Wollstonecraft's LETTERS WRITTEN DURING A
      SHORT RESIDENCE IN SWEDEN, NORWAY AND DENMARK states that
      THE MONTHLY REVIEW has many times praised Wollstonecraft
      for her strong mind. The work under review is on the whole
      commended; the descriptions of scenery and the reflections
      are singled out for special praise, together with the pas-
      sages that reveal sensibility. The faults noted are the
      labored and inelegant expression, the mixed metaphors, and
      the lack of organization.

81   THE MONTHLY REVIEW; OR, LITERARY JOURNAL, XXVII, September -
      December 1798, 321-324.

      In the review of Godwin's MEMOIRS the reviewer notes that
      Godwin wrote the MEMOIRS from pure motives, but he regrets
      the publication of the work, which should have been buried
      in oblivion. The most shocking events related in the MEM-
      OIRS are summarized; Wollstonecraft is referred to as an
      unfortunate female.

82   THE MONTHLY REVIEW; OR, LITERARY JOURNAL, XXVII, September -
      December 1798, 325-327.

      The review of Wollstonecraft's POSTHUMOUS WORKS concentrates
      on the novel, THE WRONGS OF WOMAN: OR MARIA and the view of
      marriage put forward in it. The evils Wollstonecraft por-
      trays are not considered an argument against marriage and the
      bad conduct of the husband is not judged a justification for
      the subsequent conduct of the wife. The reviewer does not
      admire the moral tendency of the book.

83   THE MONTHLY VISITOR, AND ENTERTAINING POCKET COMPANION, I,
      April 1797, 381-384.

      In a section devoted to Godwin, there is some satirical com-
      ment on his marriage to Wollstonecraft.

84 THE MONTHLY VISITOR, AND ENTERTAINING POCKET COMPANION, II,
    October 1797, 340-343.

    Some of the circumstances of Wollstonecraft's life are given;
    there is a short description of a party attended by Wollstone-
    craft and Godwin.

85 THE MONTHLY VISITOR, AND ENTERTAINING POCKET COMPANION, III,
    February 1798, 109-124.

    In a review of Godwin's MEMOIRS, a brief sketch of Wollstone-
    craft's life is given. Her irregular relationship is vindi-
    cated. The review is continued in III, March 1798, 236-242,
    where Wollstonecraft's character and writing are praised.

86 THE MONTHLY VISITOR, AND ENTERTAINING POCKET COMPANION, III,
    March 1798, 245-250.

    A letter objects to Godwin's presentation of Wollstonecraft
    as opposed to Christianity. The writer cites Wollstonecraft's
    early work, THOUGHTS ON THE EDUCATION OF DAUGHTERS and her
    late work LETTERS WRITTEN . . . IN SWEDEN as proof of her be-
    lief in immortality. Godwin should write a new conclusion to
    his MEMOIRS.

87 THE MONTHLY VISITOR, AND ENTERTAINING POCKET COMPANION, III,
    March 1798, 311-318.

    The review of POSTHUMOUS WORKS praises some aspects of THE
    WRONGS OF WOMAN. It criticizes Godwin's revelation of cer-
    tain relationships and events of Wollstonecraft's life.

88 MORNING CHRONICLE AND LONDON ADVERTISER, September 12, 1797.

    This is an obituary of Wollstonecraft. It mentions her famous
    literary works and her vigorous understanding.

89 Murray, Judith Sargeant. THE GLEANER. A MISCELLANEOUS PRO-
    DUCTION. Boston: I. Thomas and E. T. Andrews, 1798.

    Judith Sargeant Murray describes American women as already
    improving on the opinions of Wollstonecraft for they are
    ready to contend for the quantity, as well as the quality,
    of the female mind.

90 NEW ANNUAL REGISTER, OR GENERAL REPOSITORY OF HISTORY, POLI-
    TICS, AND LITERATURE, FOR THE YEAR 1790, 237.

    A short paragraph describes Wollstonecraft's VINDICATION OF
    THE RIGHTS OF MEN. It is stated that the just sentiments and
    lively ideas reveal the author as an ardent lover of liberty
    and humanity. Mention is made of Wollstonecraft's numerous
    digressions.

91   NEW ANNUAL REGISTER, OR GENERAL REPOSITORY OF HISTORY, POLI-
      TICS, AND LITERATURE, FOR THE YEAR 1792, 298.

      A review of A VINDICATION OF THE RIGHTS OF WOMAN describes
      the work as a treatise on female education which combines
      objectionable, fanciful opinions with judicious reasoning.
      The style is considered elegant and flowing. The reviewer
      recommends the book to men as well as women.

92   NEW ANNUAL REGISTER, OR GENERAL REPOSITORY OF HISTORY, POLI-
      TICS, AND LITERATURE, FOR THE YEAR 1794, 221-222.

      The reviewer of AN HISTORICAL AND MORAL VIEW OF THE ORIGIN
      AND PROGRESS OF THE FRENCH REVOLUTION considers Wollstone-
      craft a writer with a vigorous and well informed mind. The
      reflections in her work are regarded as judicious and phil-
      osophical. The style is described as impressive except in
      passages marred by excessive metaphorical language.

93   NEW ANNUAL REGISTER, OR GENERAL REPOSITORY OF HISTORY, POLI-
      TICS, AND LITERATURE, FOR THE YEAR 1796, 248-249.

      In a section entitled "Biographical Anecdotes and Characters,"
      there is a short account of Wollstonecraft's LETTERS WRITTEN
      DURING A SHORT RESIDENCE IN SWEDEN, NORWAY, AND DENMARK. The
      style of the book is described as easy and lively but not al-
      ways correct; the reflections are considered sensible, but
      sometimes too fanciful. The reviewer praises Wollstonecraft's
      pictures of nature and of men and manners, and mentions the
      melancholy tone of some passages of the work.

94   NEW ANNUAL REGISTER, OR GENERAL REPOSITORY OF HISTORY, POLI-
      TICS, AND LITERATURE, FOR THE YEAR 1798, 271.

      In a review of Godwin's MEMOIRS, Wollstonecraft is criticized
      for her licentiousness and lack of feminine modesty, although
      it is conceded that she had genius. The book is considered a
      disgusting work.

95   THE NEW-YORK MAGAZINE; OR LITERARY REPOSITORY, IV, 1793, 77-
      81.

      The introduction to Wollstonecraft's VINDICATION OF THE RIGHTS
      OF WOMAN is quoted. Wollstonecraft is described as having
      with great success vindicated the rights of woman.

96   THE NEW-YORK MAGAZINE; OR LITERARY REPOSITORY, NEW SERIES,
      II, 1797, 23-25.

      The excerpt from Wollstonecraft's LETTERS WRITTEN DURING A
      SHORT RESIDENCE IN SWEDEN, NORWAY, AND DENMARK is entitled
      "Account of the Peasantry of Norway."

97   OBSERVER, April 16, 1797.

There is reference to Godwin, the author of a pamphlet against matrimony, and his recent marriage to the lady who wrote to support the rights of woman. See Pollin, 992.

98   ORACLE AND PUBLIC ADVERTISER, April 18, 1797.

There is reference to Wollstonecraft's novel, THE WRONGS OF WOMAN, said to be nearing completion.

99   ORACLE AND PUBLIC ADVERTISER, April 20, 1797.

There is satirical reference to the philosophical marriage of Wollstonecraft and Godwin.

100   ORACLE AND PUBLIC ADVERTISER, September 16, 1797.

Wollstonecraft is described as having nearly completed a political pamphlet just before her death. Godwin is considered able to finish this work.

101   Polwhele, Rev. Richard. THE UNSEX'D FEMALES; A POEM, ADDRESSED TO THE AUTHOR OF THE PURSUITS OF LITERATURE. London, 1798.

In his poem in heroic couplets, Polwhele treats Wollstonecraft as the epitome of radical and unfeminine women infected by French principles. She is referred to as the arch-priestess of female libertinism. The facts of Wollstonecraft's life which Polwhele uses in his attack clearly derive from Godwin's MEMOIRS. Polwhele ends his poem with the fervent wish that "Mrs. Godwin" and he who drew "her frailties from their dread abode" may be numbered among "the penitent."

102   PROTESTANT DISSENTER'S MAGAZINE, 5, 1798, 148-152.

A passage concerning Wollstonecraft's religion is the same as that printed in THE MONTHLY VISITOR (See 86). It uses Wollstonecraft's early work to refute Godwin's assertions of her scepticism.

103   ROBERT AND ADELA: OR THE RIGHTS OF WOMEN BEST MAINTAINED BY THE SENTIMENTS OF NATURE. London: 1795.

This epistolary novel is written to expose the danger of the theories concerning female emancipation expressed in A VINDICATION OF THE RIGHTS OF WOMAN. Lady Susan is a young woman full of such advanced theories; she opposes marriage because it destroys independence. At the end of the book she is discomforted and brought to her senses. In the course of the book, one character expresses the opinion that"Mrs. Woolstone Croft" would never have written the book if she had been a happy wife and mother.

104 Salzmann, Christian Gotthilf. RETTUNG DER RECHTE DES WEIBES,
     MIT BEMERKUNGEN UEBER POLITISCHE UND MORALISCHE GEGENSTANDE
     VON MARIA WOLLSTONECRAFT. Schnepfenthal bei Gotha, 1793.

     In his preface, Christian Gotthilf Salzmann states his agree-
     ment with many of Wollstonecraft's sentiments as they are ex-
     pressed in A VINDICATION OF THE RIGHTS OF WOMAN. On the
     whole, however, he tones down these sentiments.

105 Salzmann, Christian Gotthilf. Preface to DENKSCHRIFT AUF
     MARIA WOLLSTONECRAFT GODWIN, DIE VERTHEIDIGERIN DER RECHTE
     DES WEIBES, VON WILLIAM GODWIN. . . . Schnepfenthal, im Ver-
     lage der Buchhandlung der Erziehungsanstalt, 1799.

     The preface is a sympathetic account of Wollstonecraft.

106 SCIENTIFIC OR FREEMASON'S MAGAZINE, X, June 1798, 403-404.

     The review of Godwin's MEMOIRS finds the work unimportant.
     Wollstonecraft is revealed more fully in her own writings.
     She provides rather a warning than a model for others. Ref-
     erence is made to her love affairs and her attempted suicide.
     The reviewer ends by declaring that surely she stands out as
     an example of misery and immorality. See Pollin 1107.

107 SCOTS MAGAZINE; OR, GENERAL REPOSITORY OF LITERATURE, HISTORY,
     AND POLITICS FOR THE YEAR 1796, LVIII, 627-628.

     This extract from Wollstonecraft's LETTERS WRITTEN DURING A
     SHORT RESIDENCE IN SWEDEN, NORWAY, AND DENMARK concerns the
     condition of Norway.

108 A SKETCH OF THE RIGHTS OF BOYS AND GIRLS. London: 1792.

     This includes Wollstonecraft among its objects of attack. It
     pretends to approve her ideas on female education and emanci-
     pation.

109 SMITH, CHARLOTTE. THE YOUNG PHILOSOPHER: A NOVEL. London:
     T. Cadell, 1798.

     Charlotte Smith quotes in a footnote Wollstonecraft's descrip-
     tion of the sky in Northern countries. The description occurs
     in her LETTERS WRITTEN. . . IN SWEDEN. In her preface, Smith
     mentions Wollstonecraft, whose talents she admired and whose
     death she regretted. She defends herself against a possible
     accusation of plagiarism because of a similarity between her
     book and Wollstonecraft's WRONGS OF WOMAN.

110 Southey, Robert. Metrical introduction to Cottle's ICELANDIC
     POETRY, OR THE EDDA OF SAEMUND, 1797.

     Reference is made to Wollstonecraft's death and its effect on
     Southey. See W. Clark Durant.

23

111 STAR, April 15, 1797.

There is reference to the marriage of Wollstonecraft and Godwin. See Pollin 1135.

112 Taylor, Thomas. A VINDICATION OF THE RIGHTS OF BRUTES, London: 1792. (Gainesville, Fla.: Scholars' Facsimiles & REPRINTS,
1966).

In his advertisement, Thomas Taylor pretends agreement with
Paine and Wollstonecraft in their zeal for the rights of humanity, and he extends their arguments to include animals.
At the end of the work Taylor anticipates the extension of
rights also to vegetables, minerals, and clods of earth when
their equality has been demonstrated. In the course of his
satire, Taylor states that Wollstonecraft has proved women
equal to men in mental abilities and bodily strength.

113 THOUGHTS ON MARRIAGE AND CRIMINAL CONVERSATION WITH SOME HINTS
OF APPROPRIATE MEANS TO CHECK THE PROGRESS OF THE LATTER, COM-
PRISING REMARKS ON THE LIFE, OPINIONS, AND EXAMPLE OF THE LATE
MRS. WOLLSTONECRAFT GODWIN. London: 1799.

The pamphlet concerns Godwin's MEMOIRS and Wollstonecraft's
POSTHUMOUS WORKS. There is comment on marriage and adultery.
Wollstonecraft is presented as an example of one who spoke
out against the unjust power of the husband over the wife,
in THE WRONGS OF WOMAN. See Pollin 1727.

114 TRUE BRITON, April 12, 1797.

There is mention of the marriage of Godwin and Wollstonecraft.
It is seen as a triumph of nature over speculation for Godwin.

115 TRUE BRITON, April 14, 1797.

A passage concerns the marriage of Godwin and Wollstonecraft
and Godwin's views on marriage. Wollstonecraft is said to
have been courted by both Godwin and Opie, the painter. Her
choice shows a preference for literature over art.

116 TRUE BRITON, April 15, 1797.

There is mention of the presumed difficulties of the domestic
life of Wollstonecraft and Godwin, because of their theories.

117 TRUE BRITON, April 18, 1797.

There is comment on the separate residences of Wollstonecraft
and Godwin.

118 TRUE BRITON, September 12, 1797.

In an obituary notice of Wollstonecraft, there is comment on
her talents and on her fine character, although the system
of morals and politics she supported is deplored.

119 TRUE BRITON, September 26, 1797.

A passage refers to Wollstonecraft's peculiar behavior. There
is comment on her suicide attempts through jealousy of Imlay.

120 TRUE BRITON, October 2, 1797.

There is reference to Godwin's great grief over the death of
Wollstonecraft.

121 UNIVERSAL MAGAZINE OF KNOWLEDGE AND PLEASURE, LXXXVI, 1790.

In a list of new publications there is reference to Wollstonecraft's LETTER TO BURKE.

122 UNIVERSAL MAGAZINE OF KNOWLEDGE AND PLEASURE, XCVIII, 1796, 108-
113.

This is an excerpt from Wollstonecraft's LETTERS WRITTEN DUR-
ING A SHORT RESIDENCE IN SWEDEN, NORWAY AND DENMARK. It is entitled " A new view of the City of Copenhagen; with Observations
on the Character and Manners of the Danes."

123 Walker, George. THE VAGABOND A NOVEL. London: G. Walker, 1799.

In George Walker's novel, the vagabond meets a married woman
named Mary, who is a convert to the new doctrines of reason and
nature. The description of her mind is taken from Godwin's
description of Wollstonecraft's in his MEMOIRS. Mary is given
many of Wollstonecraft's sentiments; footnotes refer the reader
to A VINDICATION OF THE RIGHTS OF WOMAN and to Godwin's MEMOIRS.
Mary is described as a prostitute who gives herself to the vagabond and several of his friends.

124 WALKER'S HIBERNIAN MAGAZINE; OR COMPENDIUM OF ENTERTAINING
KNOWLEDGE, April 1798, 289-296.

The review of Godwin's MEMOIRS is taken from the ANALYTICAL
REVIEW.

125 West, Jane. A TALE OF THE TIMES. London: T. N. Longman and
O. Rees, 1799.

Ideas resembling Wollstonecraft's in A VINDICATION OF THE
RIGHTS OF WOMAN and Godwin's in the MEMOIRS are attacked in
the novel.

126 AMERICAN ALMANAC AND REPERTORY OF USEFUL KNOWLEDGE FOR THE
    YEAR 1837, VIII, 1837, 295.

    In an obituary of Godwin, there is mention of the MEMOIRS;
    the work is regarded as a blot on the names of both Woll-
    stonecraft and Godwin.

127 THE ANTI-JACOBIN REVIEW AND MAGAZINE: OR MONTHLY POLITICAL
    AND LITERARY CENSOR, V, 1800, 25.

    In a review of Godwin's novel, ST. LEON, it is stated that
    the sentiments of St. Leon on the subject of women are simi-
    lar to those of Wollstonecraft.

128 THE ANTI-JACOBIN REVIEW AND MAGAZINE: OR MONTHLY POLITICAL
    AND LITERARY CENSOR, V, 1800, 39-40.

    Wollstonecraft and Godwin are ridiculed for their views on
    courtship.

129 THE ANTI-JACOBIN REVIEW AND MAGAZINE: OR MONTHLY POLITICAL
    AND LITERARY CENSOR, V, 1800, 93-94.

    In a section of necrology, Wollstonecraft and Godwin's MEM-
    OIRS are discussed with great hostility. Wollstonecraft is
    called a whore, an adulteress, and a prostitute. Her life
    is considered far worse than that of Moll Flanders. The
    reviewer is aghast at Godwin's impudence at describing his
    wife as virtuous. The WRONGS OF WOMAN is briefly discussed;
    its moral is said to be that the most grievous wrong of wo-
    man is marriage and the most sacred right adultery. The
    reviewer ends by warning other women against confounding
    notoriety with celebrity.

130 THE ANTI-JACOBIN REVIEW AND MAGAZINE: OR MONTHLY POLITICAL
    AND LITERARY CENSOR, VII, 1800, 39-46.

    In a review of Elizabeth Hamilton's MODERN PHILOSOPHERS, the
    licentious philosophy of Wollstonecraft is mentioned. The
    review is continued on pp. 369-376.

131 THE ANTI-JACOBIN REVIEW AND MAGAZINE: OR MONTHLY POLITICAL
    AND LITERARY CENSOR, VII, 1801, 437.

    There is a reference to Wollstonecraft in a letter primarily
    concerning a review of Godwin's ST. LEON.

132 THE ANTI-JACOBIN REVIEW AND MAGAZINE: OR MONTHLY POLITICAL
    AND LITERARY CENSOR, IX, 1801 Appendix, 515-520.

    A satirical poem entitle "The Vision of Liberty," is an
    attack on radical thinkers. It takes the form of a vision
    of a ruined France. Among its ruins is a bloody temple, in
    which is an image of Voltaire; to this image come the Eng-
    lish radicals, including Wollstonecraft and Godwin, seated
    on an ass. Wollstonecraft is described as wearing the

breeches in her preposterous marriage with Godwin and as
exhorting women to quit their foolish modesty and indulge
in sexual language, as well as acts. A VINDICATION OF THE
RIGHTS OF WOMAN is described as a textbook for whores and
Godwin's MEMOIRS as a record of his wife's whoredoms.

133 THE ANTI-JACOBIN REVIEW AND MAGAZINE: OR, MONTHLY POLITICAL
AND LITERARY CENSOR, XV, 1803, 182-188.

In a review of A DEFENCE OF THE CHARACTER AND CONDUCT OF
THE LATE MARY WOLLSTONECRAFT GODWIN, there is a hostile
sketch of Wollstonecraft's life as it is presented in the
MEMOIRS. Wollstonecraft is described as a prostitute.

134 ATHENAEUM JOURNAL OF LITERATURE, SCIENCE, AND THE FINE ARTS,
no. 442, April 1836, 273.

The obituary of Godwin mentions his marriage to the celebrated Mary Wollstonecraft.

135 ATHENAEUM JOURNAL OF LITERATURE, SCIENCE, THE FINE ARTS,
MUSIC, AND THE DRAMA. July - December 1885, 41-42.

A review of Elizabeth Robins Pennell's MARY WOLLSTONECRAFT
GODWIN is favorable to Wollstonecraft, whose ideas, once
considered fantastic and absurd, later became commonplace.
The reviewer mentions the neglect of Wollstonecraft, and,
because of it, wishes that the Pennell biography had been
more lively and less indebted to C. Kegan Paul. There is
much praise for Godwin's MEMOIRS and for Wollstonecraft's
LETTERS TO IMLAY, seen as the most enduring monument of
her powers.

136 ATLANTIC MONTHLY: A MAGAZINE OF LITERATURE, SCIENCE, ART,
AND POLITICS, XXXVIII, July 1876, 115-116.

In a review of C. Kegan Paul's WILLIAM GODWIN: HIS FRIENDS
AND CONTEMPORARIES, there is mention of Godwin's troubled
family relations. These appear to include Wollstonecraft
and her squalid kin.

137 Baeta, H. X. EXTRACTOS DAS CARTAS DE MARY WOLLSTONECRAFT
RELATIVAS A SUECIA, NORUEGA, E DINAMARCA, E HUMA BREVE
NOTICIA DE SUA VIDA. Lisboa, 1806.

Extracts from Wollstonecraft's LETTERS WRITTEN . . . IN
SWEDEN are given, together with a summary of the events of
her life.

138 Bates, William. THE MACLISE PORTRAIT-GALLERY OF ILLUSTRIOUS
CHARACTERS. New York: Scribner and Welford, 1883.

In a section on William Godwin, there is some mention of
Wollstonecraft. Her principles are described as dangerous,
her practice incorrect, but her emotions ardent and sincere.
Special praise is given to her LETTERS . . . IN SWEDEN,

which is said to contain more soul and feeling than any other epistolary work.

139 Befoe, William. THE SEXAGENARIAN; OR, THE RECOLLECTIONS OF A LITERARY LIFE. London: F. C. and J. Rivington, 1817.

There is a hostile account of Wollstonecraft; it includes a vicious description of her suicide attempt. The principles which Wollstonecraft vindicated are described as dangerous to female virtue.

140 Berry, Mary. EXTRACTS FROM THE JOURNALS AND CORRESPONDENCE OF MISS BERRY FROM THE YEAR 1783 to 1852. Ed. Lady Theresa Lewis. London: Longmans, Green, and Co., 1866.

Mary Berry considers that Wollstonecraft's opinions in her THOUGHTS ON THE EDUCATION OF DAUGHTERS are close to Hannah More's in her work on female education.

141 BIBLIOTHEQUE FRANCAISE, 17, January 1803, 88-91.

In a section reviewing new magazines, there is mention of Wollstonecraft as Godwin's wife.

142 BIOGRAPHIE UNIVERSELLE ANCIENNE ET MODERNE. Paris: M. Michaud, 1854.

In a section on Godwin, Wollstonecraft is referred to as a woman with uncommon intellect and warmth of heart; her freedom of action was, however, beyond that allowed to women.

143 BIOGRAPHIE UNIVERSELLE ANCIENNE ET MODERNE. Paris: M. Michaud, 1854.

The section on Wollstonecraft briefly sketches her life and comments on her works. It mentions the eloquence as well as the incorrectness of her writings. Wollstonecraft's errors are said to be caused by her deficient education and her fervid imagination.

144 BIOGRAPHIE UNIVERSELLE CLASSIQUE, OU DICTIONNAIRE HISTORIQUE PORTATIF. Paris: Charles Gosselin, 1829.

The biographical sketch of Wollstonecraft follows Godwin's MEMOIRS.

145 BIOGRAPHIE UNIVERSELLE, OU DICTIONNAIRE HISTORIQUE, CONTENANT LA NECROLOGIE DES HOMMES CELEBRES DE TOUS LES PAYS. . . Paris, 1838.

An article on Wollstonecraft summarizes her life and comments briefly on her works.

146 BIOGRAPHIE UNIVERSELLE OU DICTIONNAIRE HISTORIQUE DES HOMMES QUI SE SONT FAIT UN NOM. Paris: J. Leroux, Jouby et Ce, 1848.

Wollstonecraft's life is sketched. There is mention of her passion for Fuseli but her liaison with Imlay is ignored. Her main works are listed.

147 Bisset, Robert. DOUGLAS; OR, THE HIGHLANDER. London: C. Chapple, 1800.

Wollstonecraft's VINDICATION OF THE RIGHTS OF WOMAN is seen as a corrupting influence on young girls. Godwin's MEMOIRS are satirized.

148 Blind, Mathilde. NEW QUARTERLY MAGAZINE, July 1878.

Mathilde Blind states that, although Wollstonecraft's writings are little known, the spirit animating them has become part of the thought of a later age; many of Wollstonecraft's theories are being put into practice.

149 Bolles, John A. "Mary Wollstonecraft," HARPER'S NEW MONTHLY MAGAZINE, November 1867, 737-740.

John A. Bolles states that Wollstonecraft is almost forgotten. Reference is made to her life and to the MEMOIRS, which are considered harmful to her memory. Bolles is especially critical of her lack of religion; he states that she had no religious training at home and that she grew up substantially a pagan. A VINDICATION OF THE RIGHTS OF WOMAN is described as bold and original in its time, but the ideas became commonplace. Its composition is considered crude and its attack on abuses insolent. Wollstonecraft's life and works can serve as a warning to others.

150 Bowles, John. REFLECTIONS ON THE POLITICAL AND MORAL STATE OF SOCIETY, AT THE CLOSE OF THE EIGHTEENTH CENTURY. London: F. and C. Rivington, 1800.

John Bowles attacks certain philosophers, clearly Wollstonecraft and Godwin, who have corrupted principle and rendered the marriage tie contemptible by their teachings and by their open adultery.

151 Bowne, Eliza Southgate. A GIRL'S LIFE EIGHTY YEARS AGO: SELECTIONS FROM THE LETTERS OF ELIZA SOUTHGATE BOWNE. Introduction by Clarence Cook. New York: Charles Scribner's Sons, 1887.

In a letter of 1801, Eliza Southgate Bowne expresses qualified approval for Wollstonecraft. She considers that prejudice against Wollstonecraft has obscured her real merit. Bowne declares her admiration for many of Wollstonecraft's sentiments and for her style. She considers, however, that Wollstonecraft's life was misguided and that it is the best comment on her writings.

152 Brightwell, Cecilia Lucy. MEMORIALS OF THE LIFE OF AMELIA OPIE. Norwich: Fletcher and Alexander, 1854.

Mary Wollstonecraft is briefly mentioned. She is described as a strange, incomprehensible, woman, whose influence was to be feared. Cecelia Brightwell prints a letter from Wollstonecraft to Amelia Opie.

153 BRITISH CRITIC, XXI, June 1803, 690-691.

In a review of A DEFENSE OF THE CHARACTER AND CONDUCT OF THE LATE MARY WOLLSTONECRAFT GODWIN, Wollstonecraft is criticized for her irregularities. She is described as a whore, who should now pass into oblivion.

154 Brown, Thomas. WANDERER IN NORWAY, WITH OTHER POEMS. London: J. Murray, 1816.

The title poem of Thomas Brown's collection was inspired by Wollstonecraft's LETTERS WRITTEN . . . IN SWEDEN.

155 Browne, William Hardcastle. FAMOUS WOMEN OF HISTORY. Philadelphia: Arnold and Company, 1895.

The entry for Wollstonecraft mentions her difficult childhood, her marriage with Godwin, and her suicide attempts. She is said to have been affected throughout her life by the brutal treatment received when a child from her father.

156 Browning, Robert. "Mary Wollstonecraft and Fuseli," JOCOSERIA. THE COMPLETE WORKS OF ROBERT BROWNING. New York: Kelmscott Society, 1898.

Browning's short monologue is given to Wollstonecraft and addressed to Fuseli. It expresses Wollstonecraft's love as well as the strength and will behind it. It ends with the admission that the love has had no effect on Fuseli.

157 Burton, F. THE TIMES, January 7, 1885.

This is a reply by Sir F. Burton to C. Kegan Paul's letter written in THE TIMES, in which he·doubted the authenticity of the National Portrait Gallery's painting of Wollstonecraft. Burton gives his reasons for concluding that the Gallery picture was the one painted by John Opie for Godwin.

158 CASKET, FLOWERS OF LITERATURE, WIT & SENTIMENT, V, 1830, 14-17.

The passage starts with a consideration of Frances Wright, who is said to be a follower of Wollstonecraft. A biographical sketch of Wollstonecraft is given. She is praised for her sincerity and enthusiasm, but criticized for the language of A VINDICATION OF THE RIGHTS OF WOMAN and for its indelicate sentiments. Her book is described as a medley of reasoning and rhapsody. The reviewer states that

it is painful to contemplate such a perversion of understanding and such prostitution of ability as Wollstonecraft
reveals. The life of Wollstonecraft is seen as a lesson
on the corrupting tendency of the opinions she held.

159 CHAMBERS'S ENCYCLOPAEDIA: A DICTIONARY OF UNIVERSAL KNOW-
LEDGE FOR THE PEOPLE. London: W. and R. Chambers, 1868.

In the entry for Godwin, it is stated that he adopted and
defended Wollstonecraft's extreme social views.

160 Channing, William Ellery. MEMOIR OF WILLIAM ELLERY CHANNING.
Boston: Wm. Crosby and H. P. Nichols, 1848.

A short section concerns Wollstonecraft. She is considered
exalted and noble in her theory but dangerous to society
in her practice.

161 CHRISTIAN OBSERVER, CONDUCTED BY MEMBERS OF THE ESTABLISHED
CHURCH, I, May 1802, 303-4.

In a section entitled "Infidelity Brought to the Test of
Experiment," Wollstonecraft's life is summarized in a hostile manner with emphasis on the Imlay relationship, the
suicide attempt and the atheist death. She is given as an
example to others of the pursuit of sensual luxury instead
of the lasting pleasures of religion.

162 Clough, Emma Rauschenbusch. A STUDY OF MARY WOLLSTONECRAFT.
London: Longmans, Green, and Co., 1898.

Emma Rauschenbusch Clough summarizes Wollstonecraft's life.
She then studies the literary works in which she sees mani-
fested unusual versatility of mental powers. Finally she
comes to a consideration of Wollstonecraft's ideas, religious, ethical, political, social, and pedagogical. In
addition she considers in detail Wollstonecraft's views on
women, the causes of their intellectual and moral inferior-
ity, and the educational means that can overcome it. A
chapter concerns the relation of Wollstonecraft's views to
those of William Godwin and later socialists. Another discusses the reception of Wollstonecraft's work in Germany.

163 COLUMBIAN CENTINEL. MASSACHUSETTS FEDERALIST, XXXIV,
January 14, 1801, 1.

In a satirical poem entitled "The Enlightened Eighteenth
Century; or the Age of Reason," Wollstonecraft is mocked,
along with Godwin.

164 COLUMBIAN CENTINEL. MASSACHUSETTS FEDERALIST, XXXIV,
January 24, 1801, 1.

Wollstonecraft's works are described as dangerous. Woll-.
stonecraft is said to be an eccentric genius, who was led
away by her visionary fancy. A VINDICATION OF THE RIGHTS

OF WOMAN has many just principles and so is doubly dangerous. THE WRONGS OF WOMAN is said to have pathetic scenes
but to be poisonous in its principles. The MEMOIRS fail
as a justification of Wollstonecraft.

165 COLUMBIAN CENTINEL. MASSACHUSETTS FEDERALIST, XXXIV,
     February 14, 1801, 1.

     A letter regrets the widespread dissemination of Wollstone-
     craft's principles. Hannah More is regarded as a more pro-
     per author for women to read.

166 COLUMBIAN CENTINEL. MASSACHUSETTS FEDERALIST, XXXIV,
     February 25, 1801, 1.

     Wollstonecraft's philosophy is mocked.

167 CONDITION, INFLUENCE, RIGHTS AND APPEAL OF WOMEN. Albany,
     1845. 3rd edition used.

     Part of Wollstonecraft's VINDICATION OF THE RIGHTS OF WOMAN
     is printed, along with selections on women by writers such
     as William Thompson and John Milton.

168 Cone, Helen Gray and Jeannette L. Gilder, ed. PEN-PORTRAITS
     OF LITERARY WOMEN. New York: Cassell & Co., 1887.

     Helen Gray Cone provides a biographical sketch of Mary Woll-
     stonecraft, based primarily on C. Kegan Paul and Elizabeth
     Pennell. She disagrees with Kegan Paul's description of
     Wollstonecraft as Imlay's wife. The sketch is favorable to
     Wollstonecraft, who is seen as important because she is the
     first professional literary woman, the author of A VINDICA-
     TION OF THE RIGHTS OF WOMAN, and the writer of heart-break-
     ing letters to Imlay. The extracts presented are primarily
     from THE RIGHTS OF WOMAN and from Wollstonecraft's letters.

169 Conway, Moncure Daniel. LIFE OF THOMAS PAINE. New York:
     Putnam's Sons, 1892.

     Wollstonecraft is listed among Paine's associates in Paris
     in 1793.

170 THE CRITIC: A WEEKLY REVIEW OF LITERATURE AND THE ARTS, XV,
     1891, 39.

     A review concerns the republication of Wollstonecraft's
     VINDICATION OF THE RIGHTS OF WOMAN. It is stated that Woll-
     stonecraft's ideas and her strictures seem true even though
     the position of women has much improved. The reviewer con-
     siders that Wollstonecraft deals in a masterly way with
     popular prejudices and absurd distinctions, and her book
     is described as remarkable.

171 Cunningham, Allan. BIOGRAPHICAL AND CRITICAL HISTORY OF
THE BRITISH LITERATURE OF THE LAST FIFTY YEARS. Paris:
Baudry's Foreign Library, 1834.

In a section on Godwin, Allan Cunningham praises his
MEMOIRS of Wollstonecraft.

172 Cunningham, Allan. LIVES OF THE MOST EMINENT BRITISH
PAINTERS, SCULPTORS, AND ARCHITECTS. London: John Murray,
1829-33.

In the section on Fuseli, Wollstonecraft is mentioned.
Allan Cunningham briefly describes the "ridiculous advances"
of Wollstonecraft to Fuseli and his equally ridiculous en-
couragement of them. Wollstonecraft's life is called crazy
and vicious.

173 Davis, Matthew L. MEMOIRS OF AARON BURR. New York: Harper
& Bros., 1836.

Matthew Davis mentions Aaron Burr's admiration of A VINDI-
CATION OF THE RIGHTS OF WOMAN.

174 DEFENSE OF THE CHARACTER AND CONDUCT OF THE LATE MARY
WOLLSTONECRAFT GODWIN, FOUNDED ON PRINCIPLES OF NATURE AND
REASON, AS APPLIED TO THE PECULIAR CIRCUMSTANCES OF HER
CASE; IN A SERIES OF LETTERS TO A LADY. London: James
Wallis, 1803.

This pamphlet is a defence of Mary Wollstonecraft, although
the author is not in agreement with several of her opinions.
Wollstonecraft's character is the main object of   vindication; she is called "a virtuous and amiable woman who has
been highly calumniated." The author sees in her genuine
benevolence, enlarged philanthropy, solicitude for the in-
terests of her fellow-creatures and deference to the dic-
tates of duty. The world is found unworthy of Wollstonecraft and the author concludes that, in loftiness of spirit,
clearness of intellect, purity of intention, and benevolence
of heart, she surpasses all other people.

175 DICTIONARY OF GENERAL BIOGRAPHY by William L. R. Cates.
London: Longmans, Green and Co., 1885.

A short entry on Wollstonecraft gives a garbled version of
her life.

176 Dowden, Edward. THE FRENCH REVOLUTION AND ENGLISH LITERA-
TURE. London: Kegan Paul & Co., 1897.

Edward Dowden sees the calamities of Wollstonecraft's life
as due to the new ethics playing on an impulsive and sensitive heart. He considers A VINDICATION OF THE RIGHTS OF
WOMAN an assertion both of the claims of women and of the
claims of reason. The convictions of the book are, he
states, given imaginative embodiment in THE WRONGS OF WO-

MAN; OR MARIA. A note concerns AN HISTORICAL AND MORAL VIEW. . . OF THE FRENCH REVOLUTION, whose optimism is stressed.

177 Dowden, Edward. LIFE OF PERCY BYSSHE SHELLEY. London: Kegan Paul & Co., 1886.

Mary Wollstonecraft is mentioned several times as the mother of Mary Godwin.

178 DUBLIN UNIVERSITY MAGAZINE, LXXIII, June 1869, 672-676.

An account entitled "Mary Wolstonecraft Godwin," sketches Wollstonecraft's life according to Godwin's MEMOIRS. The writer states that the impression left by this life is not pleasant and that it is to be regretted that Wollstonecraft did not use her talents to produce more profitable results. Godwin's account of Wollstonecraft's death is especially deplored.

179 ECCENTRIC BIOGRAPHY; OR, MEMOIRS OF REMARKABLE FEMALE CHARACTERS, ANCIENT AND MODERN. Worcester: Isaiah Thomas, June, 1804.

A summary of Wollstonecraft's life is provided. She is praised for her vivacity, resolution, and for her heroic friendship. The liaison with Imlay is regarded as a marriage on Wollstonecraft's side, and the relationship with Godwin is praised. The writer is enthusiastic over Wollstonecraft and comments on her talents, understanding, and sensibility.

180 ECLECTIC MAGAZINE OF FOREIGN LITERATURE, SCIENCE, AND ART, XLII, 1885, 100-107.

An essay entitled "Mary Wollstonecraft Godwin" primarily concerns her life. It quotes from her letters and works. A VINDICATION OF THE RIGHTS OF WOMAN is judged to be disorganized, shrill, and unnecessarily long. Nonetheless, its main ideas are considered in the main true and just. THE LETTERS WRITTEN . . . IN SWEDEN is said to have charm and to have retained its interest.

181 ELIOT, GEORGE. "Margaret Fuller and Mary Wollstonecraft," LEADER, VI, October 1855, 988-989.

The article concerns Margaret Fuller's work, which is compared with Wollstonecraft's VINDICATION OF THE RIGHTS OF WOMAN. George Eliot mentions the prejudice against Wollstonecraft's book and finds it surprising considering the severely moral and serious nature of the work. Eliot finds little of literary value in Wollstonecraft, but she praises some ideas of THE RIGHTS OF WOMAN, especially the one concerning the subjection of men to ignorant and feeble-minded women. She approves also Wollstonecraft's pictures of what women are as well as what they may become.

182 Elwood, Anne Katherine. MEMOIRS OF THE LITERARY LADIES OF
     ENGLAND FROM THE COMMENCEMENT OF THE LAST CENTURY. London,
     1843.

     The events of Wollstonecraft's life are related and her
     errors blamed on defective education and unfortunate cir-
     cumstances. She is criticized for want of the feminine
     characteristics of patience and equanimity. Although
     Wollstonecraft is held to be devout, her religion is seen
     as a matter of taste and feeling only. Anne Elwood gives
     a sympathetic account of Wollstonecraft's life and assesses
     A VINDICATION OF THE RIGHTS OF WOMAN. She finds this book
     shocking, less because of its matter than because of its
     mode. The account of Wollstonecraft ends with the lament
     that a woman so gifted should, through erroneous theories
     and false principles, have become a warning rather than a
     pattern to later women.

183 Fawcett, Mrs. Henry. Introduction to A VINDICATION OF THE
     RIGHTS OF WOMAN, by Mary Wollstonecraft. New York: Scrib-
     ner and Welford, 1890.

     In her introduction, Mrs. Henry Fawcett relates Wollstone-
     craft to the women's movement. She sees her as a product
     of this movement as much as its earliest confessor. Faw-
     cett considers that, as Wollstonecraft predicted, women
     have used their greater freedom and better education in
     caring more for their children and their domestic duties.
     Fawcett praises Wollstonecraft both for her demonstration
     of the falsity of women's complete subordination to men and
     for her understanding of the high importance of women's do-
     mestic duties. Wollstonecraft is, in Fawcett's view, a wo-
     manly woman, with strong motherly and wifely instincts.
     The main arguments of THE RIGHTS OF WOMAN are summarized.

184 Fessenden, Thomas G. THE LADIES MONITOR, A POEM. Bellows
     Falls, Vermont: Bill Blake & Co., 1818.

     Thomas G. Fessenden mentions Wollstonecraft in his poem.
     The rights of woman are described as inappropriate because
     women control through female charms. In a note, Fessenden
     quotes Mrs. West's unfavorable opinion of Wollstonecraft.

185 Field, E. M. THE CHILD AND HIS BOOK. SOME ACCOUNT OF THE
     HISTORY AND PROGRESS OF CHILDREN'S LITERATURE IN ENGLAND.
     London: Wells Gardner, Darton & Co., 1892.

     A short account of Wollstonecraft is given. She is des-
     cribed as much blamed and maligned, but much admired as
     well. A short sketch of her life is given. THOUGHTS ON
     THE EDUCATION OF DAUGHTERS is described as new and start-
     ling in its time but commonplace in a later one.

186 Fisher, George P. LIFE OF BENJAMIN SILLIMAN. New York,
     1866.

George Fisher refers to Benjamin Silliman's views on Wollstonecraft. The views are best expressed in LETTERS OF SHAHCOOLEN   (see 290).

187 FRASER'S MAGAZINE FOR TOWN AND COUNTRY, X, July 1834, 463.

A sketch of Godwin mentions his connection with Wollstonecraft. It is stated that, through his publication of the MEMOIRS, he has ensured that no such woman as Wollstonecraft will appear in our literature again.

188 Fuller, Margaret. "The Great Lawsuit; Men Versus Women," THE DIAL: A MAGAZINE OF LITERATURE, PHILOSOPHY, AND RELIGION, IV, July 1843, 1-47.

Margaret Fuller praises Godwin's MEMOIRS, as well as the marriage of Wollstonecraft and Godwin, which she considers as marking a new era.

189 Fuller, Margaret. WOMAN IN THE NINETEENTH CENTURY. London: H. G. Clarke & Co., 1845.

Margaret Fuller expresses disapproval of Mary Wollstonecraft, but considers her rich in genius. She is warm in her admiration of Godwin and his love for Wollstonecraft "in the face of the world's sentence."

190 Galibert, Leon. DICTIONNAIRE DE LA CONVERSATION ET DE LA LECTURE. Paris, 1857. Edition of 1875 used.

It is stated that Godwin's marriage to Wollstonecraft violated his principles as they are expressed in POLITICAL JUSTICE. See Pollin 3317.

191 GENERAL BIOGRAPHICAL DICTIONARY, CONTAINING A SUMMARY ACCOUNT OF THE LIVES OF EMINENT PERSONS OF ALL NATIONS. By John Gorton. London: Hunt and Clarke, 1826.

A fairly full account of Wollstonecraft is given. She is described as eccentric and fanciful, a woman of great but undisciplined natural powers. In her life she showed the danger of her theories.

192 GENERAL BIOGRAPHICAL DICTIONARY: CONTAINING AN HISTORICAL AND CRITICAL ACCOUNT OF THE LIVES AND WRITINGS OF THE MOST EMINENT PERSONS IN EVERY NATION. Ed. Alexander Chalmers. London: J. Nichols & Son, 1814.

Wollstonecraft is described as a lady of genius, but her history and opinions excite pity and scorn as well as admiration. Her passions are said to have been ungovernable and she is called a voluptuary and a sensualist. It is stated that much of the MEMOIRS and POLITICAL WORKS should have been suppressed.

193 THE GENTLEMAN'S MAGAZINE,V, new series, June 1836, 666-668.

In an obituary of Godwin, his marriage to Wollstonecraft is mentioned. She is described as a woman with a more than masculine spirit of defiance to the authority of man. The MEMOIRS is considered a work disreputable to his name and to his wife's, and its subject is termed irreligious, indelicate, and dissolute.

194 Gibbons, William. AN EXPOSITION OF MODERN SCEPTICISM, IN A LETTER ADDRESSED TO THE EDITORS OF THE FREE ENQUIRER. Wilmington, Delaware: R. Porter and Son, 1830.

The work has an Appendix containing a brief notice of the life of Wollstonecraft. A VINDICATION OF THE RIGHTS OF WOMAN is described as a medley of reasoning and rhapsody. She is treated as a casualty of radical philosophy. According to the PHILADELPHIA EVENING POST, her life affords evidence of the corrupting tendency of the opinions she endeavored to inculcate.

195 Gilchrist, Alexander. LIFE OF WILLIAM BLAKE. London: Macmillan and Co., 1880.

There is a description of Blake's engravings for Wollstonecraft's ORIGINAL STORIES.

196 Gilfillan, George. A SECOND GALLERY OF LITERARY PORTRAITS. Edinburgh: J. Hogg, 1852.

A brief account of Wollstonecraft is included.

197 GRANDE ENCYCLOPEDIE INVENTAIRE RAISONNE DES SCIENCES, DES LETTRES ET DES ARTS. Paris: H. Lamirault et Cie., 1886-1902.

The entry on Wollstonecraft contains many errors. She is said to have been the daughter of an ignorant farmer and to have left home at the age of sixteen. Her fame is primarily based on her two polemical works, A VINDICATION OF THE RIGHTS OF WOMAN and A VINDICATION OF THE RIGHTS OF MEN.

198 Grant, Anne MacVicar. LETTERS FROM THE MOUNTAINS; BEING THE REAL CORRESPONDENCE OF A LADY, BETWEEN THE YEARS 1773 and 1803. London: Longman, Hurst, Rees, and Orme, 1806.

A letter of 1794 makes reference to Wollstonecraft's VINDICATION OF THE RIGHTS OF WOMAN. It is described as being very popular in Glasgow. To Anne MacVicar Grant the book revealed an author possessing great abilities but greatly misapplying them. She considers the work very dangerous because Wollstonecraft writes with feeling and seeming piety and yet her book is contrary to scripture, reason, and common sense. Grant provides a criticism of Wollstonecraft's ideas.

199 Green, Thomas. EXTRACTS FROM THE DIARY OF A LOVER OF LITER-
ATURE. Ipswich: John Raw, 1810.

An entry of 1798 refers to Thomas Green's reading of Godwin's
MEMOIRS. He expresses amusement at love's power over Godwin.

200 Hall, Robert. "Modern Infidelity Considered, with respect to
its Influence on Society," THE ENTIRE WORKS OF THE REVEREND
ROBERT HALL. London: Holdsworth & Ball, 1832.

The sermon attacks Godwin's theories of marriage and calls his
MEMOIRS a narrative of his wife's licentious amours.

201 Hall, S. C. A BOOK OF MEMORIES OF GREAT MEN AND WOMEN OF THE
AGE, FROM PERSONAL ACQUAINTANCE. London: Virtue & Co., 1871.

S. C. Hall mentions Wollstonecraft in a section on Godwin.
He states that they believed or at least argued that wedlock
was an unbecoming lie, but changed their minds later.

202 Hamilton, Catharine J. WOMEN WRITERS: THEIR WORKS AND WAYS.
London: Ward, Lock & Co., 1892.

Wollstonecraft is mentioned in the section on Amelia Opie.
The book ADELINE MOWBRAY is said to have been suggested by
the sad history of Wollstonecraft.

203 Hamilton, Elizabeth. MEMOIRS OF MODERN PHILOSOPHERS. Bath:
G. & J. Robinson, 1804.

There appear to be several references to the doctrines of
Wollstonecraft in A VINDICATION OF THE RIGHTS OF WOMAN.
There is some ridicule of the idea of the rights of women
when espoused by the feeble-minded, but Wollstonecraft's
strictures on Rousseau in her RIGHTS OF WOMAN are commended.
Wollstonecraft is described as a sensible authoress.

204 Hazlitt, William. "My First Acquaintance with Poets," THE
LIBERAL, II, 1823, 23-46.

Hazlitt includes his own and Coleridge's brief impressions
of Wollstonecraft. The essay was reprinted in SKETCHES AND
ESSAYS, ed. W. Carew Hazlitt (London: Bell and Daldy, 1869).

205 Hazlitt, William. "On Personal Character," THE PLAIN SPEAKER:
OPINIONS ON BOOKS, MEN, AND THINGS. London: Henry Colburn,
1826.

Wollstonecraft is mentioned as opposing her view of women's
equality with men to Pope's view of their subordination.

206 Hazlitt, William. THE SPIRIT OF THE AGE: OR CONTEMPORARY
PORTRAITS. London: Henry Colburn, 1825.

Wollstonecraft is referred to in the section on Godwin.

207 Hess, David. JOH. CASPAR SCHWEIZER EIN CHARACKTERBILD AUS
DEM ZEITALTER DER FRANZOSISCHER REVOLUTION. Jena, 1881.

There is reference to Wollstonecraft's friendship with Jean
Caspard Schweizer and his wife while all three were in Paris
in 1794 (see Durant, no. 417).

208 Hill, Georgiana. WOMEN IN ENGLISH LIFE. London: Richard
Bentley & Son, 1896.

Wollstonecraft and Condorcet are considered the initiators
of the women's suffrage movement.

209 Inchbald, Elizabeth. MEMOIRS OF MRS. INCHBALD. Ed. James
Boaden. London: Richard Bentley, 1833.

In a letter of 1797, Elizabeth Inchbald provides a description of Wollstonecraft's death.

210 Ingram, John H. "The Life of Mary Wollstonecraft Godwin,"
ATHENAEUM JOURNAL OF LITERATURE, SCIENCE, THE FINE ARTS,
MUSIC, AND THE DRAMA, July - December, 1885, 113.

John H. Ingram defends himself against the charges of Elizabeth Robins Pennell (see no. 267). He states that Pennell
knew in advance that changes were to be made in her biography.

211 Jeaffreson, John Cordy. NOVELS AND NOVELISTS, FROM ELIZABETH
TO VICTORIA. London: Hurst and Blackett, 1858.

A chapter deals with Wollstonecraft. A hostile summary of
her life and works is given.

212 Jeaffreson, John Cordy. THE REAL SHELLEY. NEW VIEWS OF THE
POET'S LIFE. London: Hurst and Blackett, 1885.

There is a chapter on Wollstonecraft; it relates the events
of her life, quoting from her letters. John Cordy Jeaffreson ridicules C. Kegan Paul's attempts to suppress the story
of Wollstonecraft's love for Fuseli. The hostile reception
of A VINDICATION OF THE RIGHTS OF WOMAN is said to be due to
its charges against Englishwomen, rather than its proposals.
There is some criticism of Wollstonecraft and many strictures
on her doctrines of free love.

213 Jochmann, Carol Gustav. RELIQUIEN. Hechingen: Verlag von
Georg Egersdorff, 1836.

The work includes comments on Wollstonecraft by Carl Gustav
Jochmann's friend, Count Schlabrendorf. Wollstonecraft was
a close friend of Schlabrendorf during her time in France.

214 JOURNAL DES DEBATS, August 27, 1834, 3 - 4.

A review of DE L'EDUCATION DES MERES DE FAMILLE compares the
work with Wollstonecraft's VINDICATION OF THE RIGHTS OF WOMAN.

39

It is similar to Wollstonecraft's book only in the importance it attaches to women's role. The review finds Godwin's
MEMOIRS too candid.

215   JOURNAL GENERAL DE LA LITTERATURE DE FRANCE, V, 1802, 107.

This review of Godwin's MEMOIRS in a French translation
praises Wollstonecraft's character and works. The MEMOIRS
offer a moving picture of the miseries of her life.

216   Kent, C. B. Roylance. THE ENGLISH RADICALS, AN HISTORICAL
SKETCH. London: Longmans & Co., 1899.

Wollstonecraft is mentioned as a leading feminist of her time
and the first woman to plead boldly for the rights of women.

217   Kent, William. MEMOIRS AND LETTERS OF JAMES KENT. Boston:
Little, Brown, and Company, 1898.

James Kent's views of Wollstonecraft's VINDICATION OF THE
RIGHTS OF WOMAN are noted. He considers that Wollstonecraft
reveals great energy of mind and command of language, but
that several of her opinions are fanciful and her projects
romantic.

218   Knapp, Samuel.L. ADVICE IN THE PURSUITS OF LITERATURE,
CONTAINING HISTORICAL, BIOGRAPHICAL, AND CRITICAL REMARKS.
New York: J. K. Porter, 1832.

In his book Samuel Knapp quotes Shelley's dedication of
THE REVOLT OF ISLAM; this includes the stanza concerning
Mary Wollstonecraft.

219   Knapp, Samuel L. FEMALE BIOGRAPHY; CONTAINING NOTICES OF
DISTINGUISHED WOMEN IN DIFFERENT NATIONS AND AGES. New
York: J. Carpenter, 1834.

An entry concerns Wollstonecraft's American sister-in-law,
another Mary Wolstonecraft (sic). It is stated that she
wrote on the rights of women with as much force as her more
famous namesake, but that she had no sympathy for her religious sentiments.

220   Knowles, E. H. "Letters of Mary Wollstonecraft," NOTES AND
QUERIES, 4th Series, VI, 1870, 434.

E. H. Knowles states that he possesses the autograph letters of Wollstonecraft to Fuseli.

221   Knowles, John. THE LIFE AND WRITINGS OF HENRY FUSELI.
London: Henry Colburn and Richard Bentley, 1831.

Volume I describes the life of Henry Fuseli and gives an
account of Wollstonecraft's love for him. Knowles quotes
from letters supposedly written by Wollstonecraft to
Fuseli both before and after her stay in France.

222   LADY'S MAGAZINE, 1805, 78-83.

A letter defends Wollstonecraft and the presentation of her
in Godwin's MEMOIRS.

223   LADY'S MONITOR, I, XII, November 1801, 91-92.

The section on Wollstonecraft is entitled "Memoirs of the
late Mrs. Godwin, author of A Vindication of the Rights of
Women   (From a late London Publication)." The biographical account follows the MEMOIRS, from which there are many
quotations. The account ends with Wollstonecraft's arrival in France.

224   LADY'S MONITOR, I, XIII, November 1801, 98-99.

The biographical account of Wollstonecraft concerns the
liaison with Imlay. It quotes from the letters to Imlay,
published in POSTHUMOUS WORKS.

225   LADY'S MONITOR, I, XIV, November 1801, 106-7.

The biographical account of Wollstonecraft continues with
extracts from letters to Imlay.

226   LADY'S MONITOR, I, XV, November 1801, 115-116.

The biographical account of Wollstonecraft continues with
her letters to Imlay. Her suicide letter to Imlay is
given.

227   LADY'S MONITOR, I, XVI, December 1801, 122-123.

The final letters to Imlay are quoted. Their historical
context is given. The relationship with Godwin is described and Godwin's opinions of Wollstonecraft quoted.

228   LADY'S MONITOR, I, XVII, December 1801, 130-131.

This is the concluding section of the biographical account
of Wollstonecraft. Her death is described. The writer
assesses her work and states that, although A VINDICATION
OF THE RIGHTS OF WOMAN is Wollstonecraft's most popular
work, her HISTORICAL AND MORAL VIEW OF THE FRENCH REVOLU-
TION is a better work. The character of Wollstonecraft
is discussed. She is allowed to have had great genius and
understanding and, although she deviated from propriety,
she is said to have had firm principles. Her irregular
liaisons are explained, but not justified.

229   LADY'S MONITOR, I, XXI, March 1802, 237-238.

In a section entitled "The Beauties of the Late Mary Wol-
stoncraft Godwin (sic)," there are excerpts from A VINDI-
CATION OF THE RIGHTS OF WOMAN concerning the excellent
woman, love, maternal affection, and religion.

230 LADY'S MONITOR, I, XXIII, April 1802, 260-261.

"The Beauties of the Late Mary Wollstoncraft. Godwin (sic)"
continue with an excerpt from MARY: A FICTION concerning
Mary's character.

231 LADY'S MONITOR, I, XL, 1802, 313-315.

"The Beauties of the Late Mary Wollstoncraft. Godwin (sic)"
continue with an excerpt from MARY: A FICTION concerning
happiness.

231a LADIES' MONTHLY MUSEUM OR POLITE REPOSITORY OF AMUSEMENT
AND INSTRUCTION,II, December 1815, 301-305.

This is a biographical account of Wollstonecraft. The
writer does not justify her deviation from normal stand-
ards. During her residence at Hoxton, she made the acquaintance of Godwin but disliked him. The writer speaks
of Wollstonecraft's eccentric connection with Godwin,
parts of which are obscure. The cause of her death cannot be mentioned. Her epitaph is recorded. See Pollin
563.

232 Lecky, W. A. A HISTORY OF ENGLAND IN THE EIGHTEENTH
CENTURY. London: Longman Galls & Co., 1892.

A VINDICATION OF THE RIGHTS OF WOMAN is said to have historic value as an early feminist work.

233 THE LITERARY JOURNAL, OR UNIVERSAL REVIEW OF LITERATURE,
DOMESTIC AND FOREIGN FOR THE YEAR 1805, V, March 1805,
238-249.

In a review of Godwin's novel FLEETWOOD, it is stated that
the book is intended as an "amende honorable" for his life
of Wollstonecraft, in its rapture on wedded love. See
Pollin 603.

234 LIVES OF EMINENT AND ILLUSTRIOUS ENGLISHMEN, FROM ALFRED
THE GREAT TO THE LATEST TIMES. Ed. George G. Cunningham.
Glasgow & Edinburgh: A. Fullarton & Co., 1834-7.

Wollstonecraft is briefly discussed. There is mention of
her debt to Catherine Macaulay in her VINDICATION OF THE
RIGHTS OF WOMAN.

235 Lucas, Charles. THE INFERNAL QUIXOTE, A TALE OF THE DAY.
London, 1801.

The heroine of this satirical novel is corrupted by reading modern books with revolutionary tendencies. One of
these books is Wollstonecraft's VINDICATION OF THE RIGHTS
OF WOMAN; another is Godwin's MEMOIRS, described as the
history of his own wife's intrigues.

236   Mac-Carthy, Denis Florence. SHELLEY'S EARLY LIFE FROM
       ORIGINAL SOURCES. London: John Camden Hotten, 1872.

       There are some remarks on Wollstonecraft as the mother of
       Fanny Imlay. Fanny's fate is compared with her mother's.

237   MAGAZINE OF ART, December 1899, 24, 82-83.

       Reference is made to the portrait of Wollstonecraft by
       John Opie, painted around 1797. There is a summary of the
       dispute concerning the Opie portrait.

238   Marshall, Mrs. Julian. THE LIFE AND LETTERS OF MARY WOLL-
       STONECRAFT SHELLEY. London: Richard Bentley & Son, 1889.

       Wollstonecraft is described as the opposite of Godwin, pos-
       sessing an ardent, impulsive, Irish nature. The summary of
       her life avoids mention of any incident that might place
       her in unfavorable light. A VINDICATION OF THE RIGHTS OF
       WOMAN is regarded as a shocking book, but most of its ideas,
       once considered dangerously extreme, later became common-
       place. The frankness of expression is, however, more
       shocking in 1889 than in 1792.

239   Martineau, Harriet. AUTOBIOGRAPHY, WITH MEMORIALS BY
       MARIA WESTON CHAPMAN. London: Smith, Elder & Co., 1877.

       Harriet Martineau expresses the opinion that Wollstonecraft
       is a bad influence on others and is by no means a champion
       of woman or of her rights.

240   Mayer, Gertrude Townshend. WOMEN OF LETTERS. London:
       Richard Bentley & Son, 1894.

       In a chapter on Mary Shelley, there is a résumé of Woll-
       stonecraft's life.

241   MEMOIRS OF WILLIAM GODWIN. New York Public Library Pamph-
       let. Circa 1830.

       Wollstonecraft's writings are described as monuments of her
       moral and intellectual superiority. The lofty spirit of A
       VINDICATION OF THE RIGHTS OF WOMAN and the sweetness and
       taste of LETTERS WRITTEN IN SWEDEN are commended. Woll-
       stonecraft's many amiable qualities are listed, and she is
       described as the idol of all who knew her.

242   MERCURY AND NEW-ENGLAND PALLADIUM, XVII, January 23, 1801,
       1.

       In a satire on rationalist and radical thinkers, Wollstone-
       craft is mentioned with Godwin as a corrupter of youth.

243   MERCURY AND NEW-ENGLAND PALLADIUM, XVII, February 3, 1801,
       1.

In a section on the corruptions of literature, there is
mention of Godwin's MEMOIRS and Wollstonecraft's POSTHU-
MOUS WORKS. The writer mocks the favorable reviews of
these works.

244   MERCURY AND NEW-ENGLAND PALLADIUM, XVII, April 28, 1801, 1.

In a section primarily on Godwin, Wollstonecraft is described as his whore.

245   MERCURY AND NEW-ENGLAND PALLADIUM, XVIII, October 9, 1801,
      1.

A letter to the editor condemns the reading by young girls
of novelists such as Godwin and Wollstonecraft. Writings
of authors such as Wollstonecraft are said to create false
taste and corrupt the judgment.

246   MERCURY AND NEW-ENGLAND PALLADIUM, XVIII, March 2, 1802, 1.

In a satire entitled MORPHEUS, subtitled "The Rights of
Woman," Wollstonecraft is imagined before a crowd arguing
the rights of woman and their absolute equality with men.
There is reference to her as a strumpet.

247   MERCURY AND NEW-ENGLAND PALLADIUM, XVIII, March 5, 1802, 1.

The satire MORPHEUS continues with the presentation of Wollstonecraft before the crowd. A respectable matron describes
Wollstonecraft's abandoned character and states that she
wrote as she did because she was not loved or esteemed.

248   Miller, Samuel. A BRIEF RETROSPECT OF THE EIGHTEENTH CEN-
      TURY. New York: Triand J. Sword, 1803.

In a section on education, Samuel Miller mentions Wollstonecraft and refers to the MEMOIRS as proof of her immoral
principles. It is stated that her licentious practice ren-
ders her memory odious to every friend of virtue. Samuel
Miller finds Wollstonecraft especially horrifying because
she was immoral from principle.

249   MONTHLY REVIEW; OR LITERARY JOURNAL, ENLARGED, XXXIII,
      September 1800, 23-29.

In a review of Godwin's ST. LEON, it is suggested that Godwin modified his opinions on marriage and domesticity owing
to his marriage with Wollstonecraft. The reviewer welcomes
the change.

250   MONTHLY REVIEW: OR LITERARY JOURNAL, September-December,
      1804, 447-448.

In a review of A DEFENCE OF THE CHARACTER AND CONDUCT OF
THE LATE MARY WOLLSTONECRAFT GODWIN, the writer disagrees
with the idea expressed in the pamphlet, that persons of

great genius have a rule of morality of their own.

251 More, Hannah. MEMOIRS OF THE LIFE AND CORRESPONDENCE OF
MRS. HANNAH MORE. New York: Harper & Brothers, 1834.

A letter of 1793 from Hannah More to Horace Walpole states
that she has been pestered to read Wollstonecraft's VINDI-
CATION OF THE RIGHTS OF WOMAN; she has, however, invincibly
resolved not to read it.

252 Moore, Helen. MARY WOLLSTONECRAFT SHELLEY. Philadelphia:
J. B. Lippincott Company, 1886.

There is some description of Wollstonecraft's marriage with
Godwin. Helen Moore stresses the spiritual and moral loss
which Wollstonecraft's children sustained by her death.
There is a short sketch of Wollstonecraft's life.

253 Morley, Henry. Introduction to LETTERS WRITTEN DURING A
SHORT RESIDENCE IN SWEDEN, NORWAY, AND DENMARK by Mary
Wollstonecraft. London: Cassell's National Library, 1886.

The introduction praises Wollstonecraft's LETTERS WRITTEN
. . . IN SWEDEN.

254 Mott, James and Lucretia. LIFE AND LETTERS. Ed. Anna Davis
Hallowell. Boston: Houghton, Mifflin and Company, 1896.

In an extract from a letter Elizabeth Cady Stanton mentions
her conversation with Lucretia Mott concerning the social
theories of Wollstonecraft. A letter of 1855 expresses the
belief that Wollstonecraft and other supporters of women's
rights will one day have justice done to them.

255 NEUE ALLGEMEINE DEUTSCHE BIBLIOTHEK, L, 1800, 507-519.

In a review of Godwin's MEMOIRS, there is praise of Wollstonecraft, in spite of her female weaknesses. Wollstonecraft's life is briefly summarized.

256 Noble, James A. ACADEMY. A WEEKLY REVIEW OF LITERATURE,
SCIENCE, AND ART. July 1885, 54-55.

The review of Elizabeth Robins Pennell's MARY WOLLSTONE-
CRAFT GODWIN queries her inclusion among eminent women.
Her fame is said to be due primarily to her relationship
with Godwin and Mary Shelley. Her life is said to be more
interesting than her work. James Noble criticizes Pennell's
heavy reliance on Godwin and C. Kegan Paul and the lack of
imaginative synthesis in the work.

257 NOTES AND QUERIES, Series 5, XI, March 1879, 167.

A query concerns a death cast said to be of Wollstonecraft.
It had been offered for sale.

258   NOUVELLE BIOGRAPHIE GENERALE. Paris: Firmin Didot Freres,
       1858.

       The entry on Wollstonecraft gives a fairly full summary of
       her life. Much of the advice in A VINDICATION OF THE RIGHTS
       OF WOMAN is considered just but it is pointed out that Woll-
       stonecraft was unable to follow it. The author praises THE
       LETTERS WRITTEN . . . IN SWEDEN for the revelation of vigor-
       ous intellect.

259   Ogborne, Elizabeth. HISTORY OF ESSEX, FROM THE EARLIEST
       PERIOD TO THE PRESENT TIME. . . .   London: Longman, 1814.

       Elizabeth Ogborne states that Wollstonecraft thought she
       spent her earliest years near Epping and in Epping Forest.

260   Oliphant, Margaret. LITERARY HISTORY OF ENGLAND AT THE END
       OF THE EIGHTEENTH AND BEGINNING OF THE NINETEENTH CENTURY.
       London: Macmillan & Co., 1882.

       Margaret Oliphant gives a summary of Wollstonecraft's life.
       She stresses its hardship. A VINDICATION OF THE RIGHTS OF
       WOMAN is considered mild and reasonable in its demands, al-
       though its style is inappropriate for a later age.

261   Paul, Charles Kegan. LETTERS TO IMLAY WITH A PREFATORY
       MEMOIR. London: C. Kegan Paul, 1879.

       In his MEMOIR, Charles Kegan Paul emphasizes Mary Woll-
       stonecraft's unconventionality for her time, while assert-
       ing that her opinions are mainly those which most cultiva-
       ted women later came to hold. He tries hard to vindicate
       Wollstonecraft's memory by treating as slander accounts of
       her passion for Fuseli. Kegan Paul finds no evidence of
       this and considers that Wollstonecraft's continued friend-
       ship and correspondence with Mrs. Fuseli argue against it.
       He regards the Imlay-Wollstonecraft relationship as a mar-
       riage. The MEMOIR reveals that Wollstonecraft had been
       almost unread for eighty years and that her writing can
       still shock even in the late nineteenth century.

262   Paul, C. Kegan. "Mary Wollstonecraft. A Vindication,"
       FRASER'S MAGAZINE, June 1878, 748-762.

       This is an earlier printing of the preface to C. Kegan
       Paul's edition of LETTERS TO IMLAY by Wollstonecraft.

263   Paul, C. Kegan. THE TIMES, January 1885.

       C. Kegan Paul expresses doubt of the authenticity of the
       Opie portrait of Wollstonecraft, recently hung in the
       National Portrait Gallery. He considers the portrait a
       forgery; the face is like that of an early painting of
       Wollstonecraft but is of a woman much older.

264   Paul, C. Kegan. WILLIAM GODWIN: HIS FRIENDS AND CONTEMPOR-
       ARIES. London: Henry S. King, 1876.

       C. Kegan Paul uses the papers of the Shelley family to give
       an account of Godwin and his associates, including Mary
       Wollstonecraft. He prints many previously unpublished let-
       ters from Wollstonecraft, as well as several which concern
       her written by her sisters and friends. Wollstonecraft's
       life is related in detail. Kegan Paul considers that those
       who have only heard of Wollstonecraft will be astounded to
       observe the strong vein of piety in her early letters. He
       again stresses this piety when he discusses Wollstonecraft's
       association with the Kingsboroughs, whose daughter she was
       later accused of corrupting. The awkward elements in Woll-
       stonecraft's life are glossed over; the passion for Fuseli
       is denied and the liaison with Imlay justified. A full ac-
       count of the Wollstonecraft-Godwin marriage is given. In
       comments on Wollstonecraft's literary works, A VINDICATION
       OF THE RIGHTS OF WOMAN is described as a plea for equality
       of education and a protest against the view of woman as a
       toy of men. Its frankness of speech astounds Kegan Paul,
       as does its indelicacy in the choice of certain topics.
       The book is judged hasty and rash but vigorous and eloquent.

265   Pennell, Elizabeth Robins. "A Century of Women's Rights,"
       FORTNIGHTLY REVIEW, XLVIII, New Series, July-December 1890,
       408-417.

       The essay is written on the occasion of the republication
       of Wollstonecraft's VINDICATION OF THE RIGHTS OF WOMAN.
       Elizabeth Robins Pennell states that the book has been all
       but forgotten, but that it is of the utmost interest be-
       cause it helps toward a realization of the social changes
       since it was written and because it relates to the intellec-
       tual movement of its age. Pennell sees Wollstonecraft's
       doctrine of women's rights as the legitimate conclusion of
       British history since the Reformation. She sets THE RIGHTS
       OF WOMAN in its social and literary context; she makes a
       comparison between Condorcet and Wollstonecraft.

266   Pennell, Elizabeth Robins. LIFE OF MARY WOLLSTONECRAFT.
       London: W. H. Allen, 1885.

       The Preface states that, in the writing of the biography,
       the author has relied chiefly on Godwin's MEMOIRS of Woll-
       stonecraft and on C. Kegan Paul's PREFATORY MEMOIR to the
       LETTERS TO IMLAY. These sources have been supplemented by
       an analysis of Wollstonecraft's writings and a study of
       the period in which she lived. Elizabeth Robins Pennell
       regards Wollstonecraft as a worker in the cause of human-
       ity, who was rewarded for her work by bitter censure and
       denunciation. The biography is intended as a refutation
       of the malignant attacks on Wollstonecraft, some of which
       Pennell describes. Wollstonecraft is presented favorably

throughout the book. Pennell sees pity as her ruling passion, evident in all her dealings with her family and needy
friends. The Godwin and Imlay relationships are described
very much as in Godwin's MEMOIRS, and Pennell follows C.
Kegan Paul in her effort to free Wollstonecraft from charges of immorality. Wollstonecraft's works are summarized
and assessed.

267   Pennell, Elizabeth Robins. "The Life of Mary Wollstonecraft,"
      ATHENAEUM JOURNAL OF LITERATURE, SCIENCE, THE FINE ARTS, MU-
      SIC, AND THE DRAMA, July-December 1885, 80-81.

      Elizabeth Robins Pennell replies to criticism of her biog-
      raphy of Wollstonecraft. She states that the alterations
      by John H. Ingram in the English edition of her book have
      made it lose whatever life it may originally have possessed
      (see 210).

268   Pennell, Elizabeth Robins. "The Life of Mary Wollstonecraft,"
      ATHENAEUM JOURNAL OF LITERATURE, SCIENCE, THE FINE ARTS, MU-
      SIC, AND THE DRAMA, July-December 1885, 143-144.

      Elizabeth Robins Pennell continues her dispute with John H.
      Ingram concerning the publication of her biography of Woll-
      stonecraft.

269   Pennell, Elizabeth Robins. Introduction to A VINDICATION OF
      THE RIGHTS OF WOMAN by Mary Wollstonecraft. London: Walter
      Scott, 1892.

      Elizabeth Robins Pennell considers Mary Wollstonecraft the
      first of a new genus of professional literary women. She
      states that Wollstonecraft died in the fulness of her powers
      when her greatest work seemed before her. Through her early
      death, however, she escaped a second bitter disappointment
      that might have awaited her through her relationship with
      Godwin. Pennell gives short accounts of Wollstonecraft's
      literary works and those of other contemporary authors on
      women's rights. The literary merits of A VINDICATION OF THE
      RIGHTS OF WOMAN are found to be small and the teachings of
      the book conservative by later standards; in Wollstonecraft's
      time, however, these teachings were astounding. Pennell
      stresses that the basis of THE RIGHTS OF WOMAN is Wollstone-
      craft's experience.

270   PHILADELPHIA MAGAZINE, OR WEEKLY REPOSITORY OF POLITE LIT-
      ERATURE, I, no. 12, May 1818, 89-90.

      In a review of Godwin's MEMOIRS, it is stated that Woll-
      stonecraft's life illustrates the fact that even the pos-
      session of genius fails to justify the flouting of conven-
      tional morality. There is a summary of the book.

271 Pierson, Josiah. MILLENNIUM, A POEM. Rochester: Tyler & Chipman, 1831.

In the poem, the woman teaching promiscuous intercourse may be a picture of Wollstonecraft.

272 THE PORT FOLIO, 2, July 17, 1802, 224.

A satirical poem, said to be written by Godwin and addressed to Wollstonecraft, mocks many of their ideas, especially those on love and marriage.

273 Quack, H. P. G. DE SOCIALISTEN, PERSONEN EN STELSELS. Amsterdam, 1887.

The theories of Wollstonecraft and Godwin are discussed. (See Pollin 3869).

274 Rees, Thomas. REMINISCENCES OF LITERARY LONDON FROM 1779 to 1853. New York: Francis P. Harper, 1896.

In a description of Joseph Johnson, Wollstonecraft is mentioned as a visitor to his house.

275 THE REVOLUTION, I, 24, June 1868, 370-1.

Wollstonecraft's VINDICATION OF THE RIGHTS OF WOMAN is serialized. It continues through subsequent issues of the newspaper.

276 THE REVOLUTION, II, July 1868, 23.

A note mentions Shelley's reference to Wollstonecraft in his dedication to THE REVOLT OF ISLAM.

277 Richter, Helen. MARY WOLLSTONECRAFT. Vienna, 1897.

Helen Richter describes Wollstonecraft's life and, in opposition to C. Kegan Paul, asserts the existence of the Wollstonecraft-Fuseli relationship.

278 Rickman, Thomas Clio. THE LIFE OF THOMAS PAINE. . . London: Thomas Clio Rickman, 1819.

Wollstonecraft is mentioned among the acquaintances of Thomas Paine.

279 Rigshaw, Cincinnatus. SANS CULOTIDES. London, 1800.

This is a satire on Godwin and Wollstonecraft, among other radicals. There is abusive satire on Godwin's use of love in the MEMOIRS and verses on Wollstonecraft in Godwin's arms. (See Pollin 1687).

280　Ritson, Joseph. THE LETTERS OF JOSEPH RITSON, ESQ. Ed.
　　Sir Harris Nicolas. London: William Pickering, 1833.

　　A letter of 1797 mentions that Wollstonecraft and Godwin
　　have been married according to the rites and ceremonies of
　　the Church of England of which Godwin was supposed to have
　　been contemptuous.

281　Roberts, W. MEMOIRS OF HANNAH MORE. New York: Harper &
　　Brothers, 1834.

　　W. Roberts quotes Horace Walpole's views on Wollstonecraft.

282　Robinson, Henry Crabb. DIARY, REMINISCENCES, AND CORRES-
　　PONDENCE. Ed. Thomas Sadler. London: Macmillan & Co.,1869.

　　Henry Crabb Robinson mentions Wollstonecraft several times
　　in passing, as the friend of Mary Hays, as the translator
　　of Salzmann, and as the author of A VINDICATION OF THE
　　RIGHTS OF WOMAN. Referring in 1839 to Mary Shelley's son,
　　he mentions his illustrious ancestors, including Wollstone-
　　craft.

283　Rowan, Archilbald Hamilton. AUTOBIOGRAPHY. Dublin: Thomas
　　Tegg & Co., 1840.

　　A brief sketch of Wollstonecraft is given. Her letters are
　　quoted and her relationship with Rowan in France is described.

284　Saintsbury, George. A HISTORY OF NINETEENTH CENTURY LITERA-
　　TURE. New York: Macmillan and Co., 1896.

　　Wollstonecraft's VINDICATION OF THE RIGHTS OF WOMAN is des-
　　cribed as the complement of Godwin's "New Philosophy."
　　George Saintsbury mentions the harsh treatment Wollstone-
　　craft received in her time and gives a brief sketch of her
　　life. She is said to be curiously free from bumptiousness
　　and the general qualities of the virago.

285　Scargill, W. BLUE STOCKING HALL. New York: J. & J. Harper,
　　1828.

　　The book condemns Wollstonecraft's VINDICATION OF THE RIGHTS
　　OF WOMAN and states that it long ago went into oblivion.
　　The writer is thankful that the gross absurdities of the
　　period of the French Revolution have been abandoned.

286　Scudder, H. E. ATLANTIC MONTHLY, XXXVIII, July 1876, 115-16.

　　In a review of C. Kegan Paul's WILLIAM GODWIN: HIS FRIENDS
　　AND CONTEMPORARIES, there is some consideration of Wollstone-
　　craft and her troubled relationship with Godwin. Her unpleas-
　　ant relatives are mentioned.

287 Seward, Anna. LETTERS OF ANNA SEWARD WRITTEN BETWEEN THE
YEARS 1784 AND 1807. Edinburgh: Archibald Constable and
Company, 1811.

In a letter of 1792, Anna Seward expresses enthusiasm for
Wollstonecraft's VINDICATION OF THE RIGHTS OF WOMAN. Although considering that Wollstonecraft carried her ideas
of sexual equality too far, she felt that the remarks on
female education and its results were just. In a letter
of 1798, Seward discusses Godwin's MEMOIRS. She states
that it is the fashion to abuse Godwin, but that she finds
his work most valuable. She considers that Wollstonecraft's virtues were more in evidence than her errors. Seward justifies Wollstonecraft's conduct in regard to Imlay,
as well as Godwin's revelation of the affair. She criticizes Godwin, however, for his needless display of his religious scepticism, in which he implicated his wife.

288 Shelley, Percy Bysshe. "Revolt of Islam," THE POETICAL
WORKS OF PERCY BYSSHE SHELLEY. London: Edward Moxon, 1839.

In the dedication of "The Revolt of Islam," Percy Bysshe
Shelley addresses Mary and mentions her mother, Mary Wollstonecraft. She is said to have clothed her daughter in
her own radiance.

289 Silliman, Benjamin. THE THEORIES OF MODERN PHILOSOPHY IN
RELIGION, GOVERNMENT, AND MORALS, CONTRASTED WITH THE PRAC-
TICAL SYSTEM OF NEW ENGLAND. Hartford, 1802.

This is an attack primarily on Godwin, but Wollstonecraft
is also criticized in comment on the MEMOIRS.

290 [Silliman, Benjamin]. "Letters of Shahcoolen," COMMERCIAL
ADVERTISER, V, October 1801.

In the October edition of the COMMERCIAL ADVERTISER and in
subsequent editions, Benjamin Silliman's "Letters of Shahcoolen" are serialized. They give a hostile account of
Wollstonecraft's life as it is presented by Godwin and they
summarize Wollstonecraft's most shocking ideas. Silliman
considers Wollstonecraft a lewd woman and a lunatic, whose
ideas are dangerous and in need of refutation.

291 [Silliman, Benjamin]. LETTERS OF SHAHCOOLEN. Boston:
Russell and Cutler, 1802.

This is a reprinting, with some changes, of the series first
published in the COMMERCIAL ADVERTISER (see 290).

292 Simcox, Edith. ACADEMY: A WEEKLY REVIEW OF LITERATURE,
SCIENCE, AND ART. IX, February 1876, 115-117.

This is a review of C. Kegan Paul's WILLIAM GODWIN: HIS
FRIENDS AND CONTEMPORARIES. The section concerning Wollstonecraft is summarized. Edith Simcox finds some of Woll-

stonecraft's letters to her sisters painful. She stresses
the hardship of Wollstonecraft's life and its demoralizing
effect on her character. She detects in Wollstonecraft
something like a feminine counterpart to the obtuse exact-
ness which made Godwin a difficult friend.

293 Southey, Robert. THE CORRESPONDENCE OF ROBERT SOUTHEY WITH
     CAROLINE BOWLES. London: Longmans, Green,1881.

In a letter of 1824, Robert Southey describes Wollstonecraft
as a delightful woman, but one who attached herself to men
who were unworthy of her. He repeats this opinion in a
letter written later in the same year.

294 Southey, Robert. LIFE AND CORRESPONDENCE. Ed. Charles C.
     Southey, 1851. London: Longman, Brown, Green, and Longmans.
     1849.

In a letter to Joseph Cottle in 1797, Robert Southey states
that, among the faces of literary people he has seen, Wollstonecraft's is the best. Her expression of haughtiness is,
however, not to his taste. There is a short description of
Wollstonecraft's appearance. In a letter to John Rickman in
1800, Southey asserts that Wollstonecraft was just beginning
to reason when she died.

295 Southey, Robert. "Triumph of Woman," THE POETICAL WORKS OF
     ROBERT SOUTHEY. London: Longman, Brown, Green, and Longmans,
     1845.

In lines prefixed to the poem, Southey praises Wollstonecraft for her personal charms, as well as for her intellectual power and zeal.

296 SPECTATOR, XL, April 1876, 532-3.

This is a review of C. Kegan Paul's WILLIAM GODWIN: HIS
FRIENDS AND CONTEMPORARIES. Godwin's marriage to Wollstonecraft is discussed; it is considered the most interesting period of Godwin's life.

297 Stephen, Leslie. DICTIONARY OF NATIONAL BIOGRAPHY. Ed.
     Leslie Stephen and Sidney Lee. London: Smith, Elder & Co.,
     1890.

The entry on Wollstonecraft by Leslie Stephen gives a
sketch of her life. She is described as an impulsive and
enthusiastic woman, with great charms of person and manner.
Her books are said to show genuine eloquence although
marred by the stilted sentimentalism of the time.

The entry on Godwin includes a short account of his marriage to Wollstonecraft.

298 Stephen, Leslie. HISTORY OF ENGLISH THOUGHT IN THE EIGHT-
     EENTH CENTURY. London: Smith, Elder & Co., 1876.

     Leslie Stephen considers that Wollstonecraft's VINDICATION
     OF THE RIGHTS OF WOMAN anticipates many of the arguments
     of a later generation. He criticizes Wollstonecraft's pom-
     pous and mannered style.

299 STOREHOUSE OF STORIES. Ed. Charlotte M. Yonge. London:
     Macmillan, 1872.

     This work includes stories from Salzmann's ELEMENTS OF
     MORALITY, translated by Wollstonecraft.

300 Taine, Hippolyte A. HISTORY OF ENGLISH LITERATURE.
     New York, 1883.

     A footnote quotes from Wollstonecraft's HISTORICAL AND
     MORAL VIEW OF . . . THE FRENCH REVOLUTION.

301 Taylor, I. A. "An Eighteenth-Century Friendship," LONG-
     MAN'S MAGAZINE, XIX, February 1892, 412-425.

     The article concerns the friendship of Godwin and Mrs.
     Inchbald. It describes Inchbald's hostile reaction to
     the marriage of Wollstonecraft and Godwin. After his
     wife's death, Godwin tried unsuccessfully to resume his
     friendship with Inchbald.

302 Thompson, William. APPEAL OF ONE HALF THE HUMAN RACE,
     WOMEN, AGAINST THE PRETENSIONS OF THE OTHER HALF, MEN,
     TO RETAIN THEM IN POLITICAL, AND THENCE IN CIVIL AND
     DOMESTIC, SLAVERY. London, 1825.

     The introductory letter mentions Wollstonecraft and charges
     her with marring her pages and diminshing their usefulness
     through narrow views.

303 Ticknor, George. LIFE, LETTERS, AND JOURNALS OF GEORGE
     TICKNOR. Boston: James R. Osgood and Company, 1876.

     George Ticknor calls Wollstonecraft "notorious."

304 THE TIMES, April 16, 1836, 5.

     In an obituary of Godwin, there is mention of his burial
     near Wollstonecraft and of the state of her coffin.

305 Tristan, Flora. PROMENADES DANS LONDRES. Londres: W.
     Jeffs, 1840.

     In a chapter entitled "Les Femmes Anglaises," there is a
     discussion of Wollstonecraft.

306 Vincens, Cecile. PORTRAITS DE FEMMES. . .   Paris: Lib-
     rairie Hachette et Cie., 1887.

This book includes a sketch of Mary Wollstonecraft.

307 VIE ET MEMOIRES DE MARIE WOLLSTONECRAFT GODWIN, AUTEUR DE
LA DEFENSE DES DROITS DE LA FEMME . . . Paris: Testu, Fuchs,
Desenne, Le Prieur, Petit, 1802.

The preface gives a favorable account of Wollstonecraft,excusing her relationship with Imlay, but considering it an
example of the weakness she disliked in other women.

308 VINDICATION OF THE RIGHTS OF WOMAN. New York: A. J. Matsell,
1833.

There is a brief sympathetic sketch of Wollstonecraft's life.
According to the author, the facts are taken from Godwin's
MEMOIRS.

309 VINDICATION OF THE RIGHTS OF WOMAN. London: W. Strange,
1844.

In the introduction, the editor states that the public mind
has moved toward a juster view of the position of women than
the one held when Wollstonecraft wrote. Nonetheless, the
edition of Wollstonecraft's work is heavily edited.

310 VINDICATION OF THE RIGHTS OF WOMAN (extract). A LIBRARY OF
THE WORLD'S BEST LITERATURE ANCIENT AND MODERN. Ed. Charles
Dudley Warner. New York: The International Society, 1897.

The author of the biographical sketch prefacing the extract
considers that Wollstonecraft's experiences forced her into
extreme opinions. These opinions are, however, now truisms
and THE RIGHTS OF WOMAN is little read, although in its time
it was an epoch-making book.

311 Walpole, Horace. LETTERS OF HORACE WALPOLE. Ed. Peter Cunningham. London: Henry G. Bohn, 1861.

Walpole's letter to Hannah More contains his famous phrase
for Wollstonecraft and criticism of her for her attacks on
Marie Antoinette.

312 THE WASHINGTON FEDERALIST, I, no. 106, May 29, 1801, 3.

A letter laments the destruction of womanly virtue through
the reading of modern philosophism.Richardson and Addison
are laid aside for Godwin and Wollstonecraft, to be read by
our daughters. (See Pollin 1198).

313 West, Jane. LETTERS ADDRESSED TO A YOUNG MAN ON HIS FIRST
ENTRANCE INTO LIFE AND ADAPTED TO THE PECULIAR CIRCUMSTANCES
OF THE PRESENT TIMES. London: A. Strahan, 1801.

Several chapters warn the reader against modern philosophy.

In Letter XIII, Jane West refers to Wollstonecraft's "extravagant doctrines" and to her miserable death. She declares that the account of Wollstonecraft's last moments and the opinions expressed in her posthumous writing show her lamentable spiritual state. West quotes incorrectly from A VINDICATION OF THE RIGHTS OF WOMAN.

314 WESTMINSTER REVIEW, CXXXIII, January - June, 1890, 10-23.

The writer wishes to prove that Wollstonecraft is an original thinker, one extraordinarily in advance of her age. Her views and opinions on woman's position in the social economy and on education are said to be those put forward by all thoughtful men and women a century later. The events of Wollstonecraft's life are related, and her works briefly discussed. A VINDICATION OF THE RIGHTS OF WOMAN is described as forming an epoch in its subject. The book is summarized and its arguments related to those of John Stuart Mill. Wollstonecraft's originality is stressed.

315 WESTMINSTER REVIEW, CXXXV, January - June, 1891, 85-86.

In a section entitled "Sociology," there is comment on the edition of A VINDICATION OF THE RIGHTS OF WOMAN, edited by Mrs. Henry Fawcett in 1891. The writer expresses amazement at the condition of women in Wollstonecraft's day.

316 Wolstonecraft, Mary [sic]. "The National Rights of Woman," BOSTON MONTHLY MAGAZINE, I, August 1825, 126-35.

The article is by Wollstonecraft's sister-in-law. It is described in Durant (see 417).

317 Woodberry, George E. "Mary Wollstonecraft," ATLANTIC MONTHLY, XLVI, 1880, 838-846.

George Woodberry expresses his enthusiasm for Wollstonecraft, described as a beautiful woman, to whom the world has ungenerously refused her due of gratitude. The story of her life is worth telling because it is the story of the first vindicator of the right of women to freedom and intellectual opportunity, and the story of the first Englishwoman to make a living solely through literature. Wollstonecraft's life is seen as one of fortitude, affection, and pathos. THE RIGHTS OF WOMAN is not considered radical and the rights vindicated are described as few and primitive; it was the lack of reserve in expression that shocked. Woodberry concludes his account by stating that Wollstonecraft's only error was her error in conduct with Imlay; excepting that, it would be difficult to find in her life anything more blameworthy than rational and active liberalism.

318 Zimmern, Helen. "Mary Wollstonecraft," DEUTSCHE RUNDSCHAU, LX, 1889, 247-263.

This is a biographical sketch of Wollstonecraft. It is

based on C. Kegan Paul's PREFATORY MEMOIR to the LETTERS TO IMLAY and on his WILLIAM GODWIN: HIS FRIENDS AND CONTEMPORARIES.

319 Zschokke, Johann Heinrich Daniel. PROMETHEUS: FUR LICHT UND RECHT. Aarau, 1832.

Wollstonecraft's friendship with Count Schlabrendorf is mentioned.

320   Abrash, Barbara.   LIBRARY JOURNAL, September 1972, 2720.

In her review of Eleanor Flexner's biography of Wollstonecraft, Barbara Abrash finds the work carefully documented
and informative. Flexner is said to have succeeded well
in revealing an emotionally and intellectually complex woman.

321   Adams, John.   "Comments on Mary Wollstonecraft's French
Revolution," BULLETIN OF THE BOSTON PUBLIC LIBRARY, Series
4, V, II, January - March 1923, 4-13.

On the evidence of her book AN HISTORICAL AND MORAL VIEW OF
THE ORIGIN AND PROGRESS OF THE FRENCH REVOLUTION, John
Adams described Wollstonecraft as a lady of masculine understanding. He admired the enthusiasm with which she presented her vision of perfectibility. He differed from her
primarily in his belief in an aristocracy of merit and in
his scepticism about the absolute power of virtue.

322   Adams, M. Ray.   "Joel Barlow, Political Romanticist," AMER-
ICAN LITERATURE, IX, May 1937, 113-152.

Barlow's friendship with Wollstonecraft is mentioned.

323   Adams, M. Ray.   "Mary Hays, Disciple of William Godwin,"
PMLA, IV, II, June 1940, 472-483.

The article mentions Wollstonecraft's influence on the
theories of Mary Hays.

324   Adams, M. Ray.   STUDIES IN THE LITERARY BACKGROUNDS OF ENG-
LISH RADICALISM WITH SPECIAL REFERENCE TO THE FRENCH REVOLU-
TION. Pennsylvania: Franklin and Marshall College, 1947.

This volume reprints M. Ray Adams' essays on Mary Hays and
Joel Barlow (see 322 and 323).

325   Adelman, Joseph.   FAMOUS WOMEN, AN OUTLINE OF FEMININE
ACHIEVEMENT THROUGH THE AGES WITH LIFE STORIES OF FIVE HUN-
DRED NOTED WOMEN. New York: Ellis M. Lonow Co., 1926.

A section on Wollstonecraft describes her as the most brilliant of the advanced women of her time. A VINDICATION OF
THE RIGHTS OF WOMAN is said to be a conspicuous landmark in
the history of feminism.

326   Allen, B. Sprague.   "The Reaction Against William Godwin,"
MODERN PHILOLOGY, XVI, September 1918, 57-75.

B. Sprague Allen discusses the hostile reception of Godwin's
MEMOIRS, which, he considers, brought Wollstonecraft into
greater disrepute than ever. THE WRONGS OF WOMAN was considered proof of Godwin's radical influence on Wollstonecraft.

327 Allentuck, Marcia. "Mary Wollstonecraft," TIMES LITERARY
SUPPLEMENT, December 9, 1960, 797.

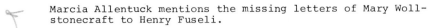

Marcia Allentuck mentions the missing letters of Mary Wollstonecraft to Henry Fuseli.

328 ART WORLD AND ARTS AND DECORATION, IX, August 1918, 226.

The portrait of Wollstonecraft by John Opie is reproduced.
Its history is briefly stated.

329 ATHENAEUM, March 18, 1911, 300.

The review of G. R. Stirling Taylor's biography of Wollstonecraft describes the book as on the whole sound, although given in some places to exaggeration. Taylor's
enthusiasm is praised.

330 Axon, William E. A. "Two Disillusionments," THE BOOKMAN,
XXXIV, 1908, 26-28.

In a review of Roger Ingpen's edition of THE LOVE LETTERS
OF MARY WOLLSTONECRAFT TO GILBERT IMLAY, William Axon
gives a brief account of Wollstonecraft's relationship
with Gilbert Imlay.

331 Baine, Rodney M. THOMAS HOLCROFT AND THE REVOLUTIONARY
NOVEL. Athens: University of Georgia Press, 1965.

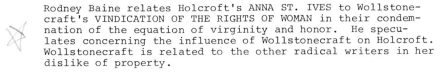

Rodney Baine relates Holcroft's ANNA ST. IVES to Wollstonecraft's VINDICATION OF THE RIGHTS OF WOMAN in their condemnation of the equation of virginity and honor. He speculates concerning the influence of Wollstonecraft on Holcroft.
Wollstonecraft is related to the other radical writers in her
dislike of property.

332 Baker, Ernest A. HISTORY OF THE ENGLISH NOVEL. London:
H. F. & G. Witherby, 1934.

Wollstonecraft's MARY, A FICTION is briefly discussed. It
is described as a heavy tribute to sensibility.

333 Barrett Browning, Elizabeth. ELIZABETH BARRETT TO MISS MIT-
FORD. Ed. Betty Miller. London: John Murray, 1954.

In a letter of 1842, Elizabeth Barrett Browning states that
she read Wollstonecraft when she was twelve.

334 Bascom, John. "The Case of Mary Wollstonecraft," THE DIAL:
A SEMI-MONTHLY JOURNAL OF LITERARY CRITICISM, DISCUSSION,
AND INFORMATION, LI, July - December 4, 1911, 76-78.

This is a review of G. R. Stirling Taylor's MARY WOLLSTONE-
CRAFT: A STUDY IN ECONOMICS AND ROMANCE. John Bascom calls

Wollstonecraft a notable character in the world's history, whose true personal and social position it has been diffi- cult to assign. He considers her marked by intellectual antagonism to such an extent that she was blind to the slow changes of reform. He adds that she overstated the claims of personal liberty and understated those of society.

335 Bass, Robert D. THE GREEN DRAGOON: THE LIVES OF BANASTRE TARLETON AND MARY ROBINSON. New York: Henry Holt & Co., Inc., 1957.

There is mention of the influence of Wollstonecraft's ideas on those of Mary Robinson.

336 Baum, Paull Franklin. "Mary Imlay," FREEMAN, VIII, 1923, 157-8.

This is a biographical account of Wollstonecraft, who is described as a faded historic figure. Her works are said to be largely forgotten. Paull Baum wishes to stress a side of her life which he considers deserves more regard than it has ever had: she is entitled to a place among the lower ranks of great lovers. The record of her love for Imlay (here called Robert) is chronicled in her letters, which are quoted.

337 Baxter, Annette K. WOMEN'S STUDIES II, I, 124-126.

This is a review of Eleanor Flexner's MARY WOLLSTONECRAFT, A BIOGRAPHY.

338 Beard, Mary R. WOMAN AS FORCE IN HISTORY: A STUDY IN TRADI- TIONS AND REALITIES. New York: The Macmillan Company, 1946.

A section on Wollstonecraft concentrates on A VINDICATION OF THE RIGHTS OF WOMAN. Beard blames Wollstonecraft for vitalizing the doctrine that married women are civilly dead and have been in history nothing but men's playthings and intriguers. Wollstonecraft should have inquired how far and in what respects the theory that women have power through men conformed to the facts of women in contemporary society and in history. Beard finds preposterous Wollstonecraft's comparison of women with soldiers. There is a summary of some of Wollstonecraft's arguments in THE RIGHTS OF WOMAN.

339 Beaty, Frederick L. LOVE IN BRITISH ROMANTIC LITERATURE. DeKalb: Northern Illinois University Press, 1971.

In a chapter on "The New Moralists," there is some discussion of Mary Wollstonecraft. Her views on contemporary marriage, as they are expressed in A VINDICATION OF THE RIGHTS OF WOMAN, are summarized.

340 Beer, Patricia. "True Delicacy," LISTENER, September 5, 1974, 314-315.

In her review of Claire Tomalin's biography of Wollstonecraft, Patricia Beer states that Wollstonecraft advocated
the impossible: sexual freedom when this would lead to
pregnancy and pregnancy frequently ended in death. Beer
compares Wollstonecraft to George Eliot in her family life
and public career.

341 Ben-Israel, Hedva. ENGLISH HISTORIANS ON THE FRENCH REVO-
LUTION. Cambridge: at the University Press, 1968.

Hedva Ben-Israel briefly discusses Wollstonecraft's HISTOR-
ICAL AND MORAL VIEW OF THE ORIGIN AND PROGRESS OF THE FRENCH
REVOLUTION. She sees as Wollstonecraft's thesis the idea
that the Revolution was the natural consequence of intellectual improvement. She finds Wollstonecraft's view, that
violence was not organic to the Revolution, shared by Mack-
intosh and later Mill and Macaulay.

342 Benedict, Ruth. "Mary Wollstonecraft," AN ANTHROPOLOGIST
AT WORK: WRITINGS OF RUTH BENEDICT, Ed. Margaret Mead.
Boston: Houghton, Mifflin, 1959.

Ruth Benedict calls Wollstonecraft's biography the story of
a life that achieved an idea. She sees Wollstonecraft pro-
testing against privilege of all kinds, of kings and men in
general. This protest, in Benedict's view, resulted from
the child's resentment at her father's arbitrary blows.
Benedict stresses that Wollstonecraft is not against marriage, which is seen as the basis of nearly all social virtue, but that she considers the first duty of women is to
themselves as rational creatures. Benedict notes the breakdown of some of Wollstonecraft's principles during the Imlay
affair.

343 Benson, Mary Sumner. WOMEN IN EIGHTEENTH-CENTURY AMERICA:
A STUDY OF OPINION AND SOCIAL USAGE. New York: Columbia
University Press, 1935.

There are many references to Wollstonecraft throughout the
book, as well as a discussion of the effect of A VINDICA-
TION OF THE RIGHTS OF WOMAN on American readers. Immediate reactions to this work were less favorable than later
ones.

344 Birley, Robert. THE ENGLISH JACOBINS FROM 1789 to 1802.
London: Oxford University Press, 1924.

Robert Birley notes Wollstonecraft's anger in her VINDICA-
TION OF THE RIGHTS OF MEN against Burke's contemptuous
attitude toward the poor.

345 Black, Frank Gees. THE EPISTOLARY NOVEL IN THE LATE EIGHT-
EENTH CENTURY. Eugene: University of Oregon, 1940.

Wollstonecraft's WRONGS OF WOMAN and her translation of
YOUNG GRANDISON are mentioned but not discussed.

346 Blease, W. Lyon. THE EMANCIPATION OF ENGLISH WOMEN.
London: David Nutt, 1913.

The chapter concerning Wollstonecraft places her within her
historical context. The French Revolution is seen as the
inspiration for A VINDICATION OF THE RIGHTS OF WOMAN. This
book is not a work of genius for it has many faults, but it
reveals a burning and fiery insight. The main theories of
THE RIGHTS OF WOMAN are summarized; stress is laid on Wollstonecraft's appreciation of the individuality of every woman
and her plea for woman's spiritual independence.

347 Bliven, Naomi. "Books: Pioneer's Progress," THE NEW YORKER,
May 26, 1975, 117-118.

This is a discussion of THE WRONGS OF WOMAN, prompted by the
Norton reprinting of the work. The novel is described as a
restatement, in fictional form, of the ideas of A VINDICATION
OF THE RIGHTS OF WOMAN. It is praised as a polemical rather
than a fictional work. The conception, if not the realization, of Jemima in the novel is especially commended, but the
treatment of the themes of money and property is considered
vague and rather implausible. Naomi Bliven states that the
novel is arguing for the legal recognition of romantic love
and she considers that Wollstonecraft is wrong in believing
such love rare and valuable.

348 Block, Andrew. THE ENGLISH NOVEL 1740 - 1850. London:
Grafton & Co., 1939.

Wollstonecraft's novel MARY, A FICTION is listed, as well as
her ORIGINAL STORIES.

349 Bloomfield, Paul. EDWARD GIBBON WAKEFIELD: BUILDER OF THE
BRITISH COMMONWEALTH. London: Longmans, Green & Company,
Ltd., 1961.

There is a short comparison of Priscilla Wakefield and Wollstonecraft.

350 Boas, Louise Schutz. Introduction to A VINDICATION OF THE
RIGHTS OF BRUTES by Thomas Taylor. Gainesville, Florida:
Scholars' Facsimiles & Reprints, 1966.

The introduction discusses the attack on Paine and Wollstonecraft.

351 BODLEIAN LIBRARY RECORD, "Notable Accessions," October 5,
1954, 109-111.

The list includes first editions of Mary Wollstonecraft's
works.

352 BOOKLIST, October, 1932, 42.

This is a note on H. R. James's biography of Wollstonecraft. The book is said to convey the impression that Wollstonecraft was greater than her works.

353 BOOK LIST, December 15, 1972, 367.

A short review of Eleanor Flexner's biography of Wollstonecraft describes Flexner's subject as a complex, often puzzling personality. The book explains the disturbing contradictions in Wollstonecraft's character and behavior by describing her difficult childhood and youth.

354 BOOK LIST, January 1, 1973, 434-435.

Eleanor Flexner's biography of Wollstonecraft is said to be a help in putting the present feminist movement in perspective.

355 BOOKMAN, LXVI, 1924, 213.

Wollstonecraft's portrait is reproduced, together with those of Scott, Keats, and Byron.

356 BOOKMAN, LXXV, 1932, 753.

This is a hostile review of James's biography of Wollstonecraft.

357 Boos, Florence. "The Biographies of Mary Wollstonecraft," MARY WOLLSTONECRAFT NEWSLETTER, I, II, April 1973, 6-10.

Florence Boos considers three recent biographies of Wollstonecraft: those by Margaret George, Ralph Wardle, and Eleanor Flexner. She concludes that Wardle's book, in comparison with Flexner's, presents something slightly closer to an official version, that is Wollstonecraft's life as seen by herself and Godwin. Flexner is more sceptical of Godwin's MEMOIRS than Wardle, and her biography creates interest by its implicit suggestion that there are still open questions of fact and bias. George's book Boos finds a highly idiosyncratic essay rather than an extended biography.

358 Borer, Mary Cathcart. WOMEN WHO MADE HISTORY. London: Frederick Warne & Co. Ltd., 1963.

Mary Borer summarizes the events of Wollstonecraft's life. She considers that her writings undoubtedly influenced social developments throughout the nineteenth century.

359 Boulton, James T. THE LANGUAGE OF POLITICS IN THE AGE OF WILKES AND BURKE. London: Routledge & Kegan Paul, 1963.

In a discussion of the language of politics in the late eighteenth century, James T. Boulton makes some comment on Wollstonecraft's RIGHTS OF MEN. He regards Wollstonecraft's

opposition to Burke as humanitarian; she identifies herself
with the poor and considers Burke's inability to do so as a
failure of reason. Wollstonecraft sees her attack on Burke
as the assault of a rationalist on an imaginative and sentimental writer, out of place in a world of politics. Boulton
finds the vigor of Wollstonecraft's work refreshing, but he
considers that the lack of organization severely weakens her
denunciation of the REFLECTIONS for the same defect. Wollstonecraft's style frequently seems inappropriate for her
message.

360 Boyle, F. A. LIBRARY JOURNAL, September 15, 1951, 1423.

This is a short, favorable review of Ralph Wardle's biography of Wollstonecraft.

361 Bradbrook, Frank W. JANE AUSTEN AND HER PREDECESSORS. Cambridge: at the University Press, 1967.

Frank W. Bradbrook states that Jane Austen despised the ex-
treme feminism of the Wollstonecraft type. He mentions
Wollstonecraft's attack on Dr. Fordyce's SERMONS TO YOUNG
WOMEN.

362 Brailsford, H. N. SHELLEY, GODWIN, AND THEIR CIRCLE. 1913;
Archon Books, 1969.

H. N. Brailsford summarizes Mary Wollstonecraft's life,
glossing over the problematical episodes. He expresses his
enthusiasm for her character and sees her as a good sister,
an affectionate friend and a devoted and tender mother. He
stresses her relevance for the women's movement of his own
time and relates A VINDICATION OF THE RIGHTS OF WOMAN to
earlier works on women's emancipation. Brailsford discusses
THE RIGHTS OF WOMAN, finding it a faulty though an intensely
vital performance and seeing it rooted strongly in Wollstonecraft's experience. He links the ideas expressed in the book
with the ideas of the revolutionary movement in general.

363 Briggs, Asa. SCIENCE AND SOCIETY, XXXV, Fall 1971, 370-372.

In a review of Margaret George's biography Asa Briggs describes Wollstonecraft as one of the key figures in the tran-
sitional but also revolutionary period between the Enlightenment and the advent of socialism. Briggs praises Wollstonecraft for her sense of the suffering of other people,
acquired through her own suffering.

364 BRITISH HISTORICAL PORTRAITS: A SELECTION FROM THE NATIONAL
PORTRAIT GALLERY WITH BIOGRAPHICAL NOTES. Cambridge: at
the University Press, 1957.

The work includes a portrait of Wollstonecraft.

365 BROCKHAUS' KONVERSATIONS-LEXIKON. Leipzig: F. A. Brockhaus, 1902.

There is a short summary of Wollstonecraft's life.

366 Brown, Ford K. THE LIFE OF WILLIAM GODWIN. London: J. M. Dent & Sons, 1926.

Ford K. Brown describes Wollstonecraft's relationship with Godwin; he presents the first meeting and the final relationship and marriage. He is especially detailed on the reactions of Godwin's women friends to the Wollstonecraft-Godwin marriage. In the course of his account of the marriage he quotes liberally from the letters of Wollstonecraft and Godwin, as well as from letters and accounts of contemporaries such as Southey.

367 Brown, F. K. HERALD TRIBUNE, August 21, 1927, 3.

In a review of Durant's edition of Godwin's MEMOIRS, F. K. Brown praises the work for its emotional tone and for its presentation of Wollstonecraft.

368 Brown, Philip Anthony. THE FRENCH REVOLUTION IN ENGLISH HISTORY. London: Frank Cass, 1965.

Philip Brown discusses A VINDICATION OF THE RIGHTS OF MEN as an answer to Burke's REFLECTIONS. It is said to have the virtue and vice of high-pressure writing: it is charged with emotion and is unfair and disordered.

369 Brownmiller, Susan. NEW YORK TIMES BOOK REVIEW, October 1972, 4.

In her review of Eleanor Flexner's biography, Susan Brownmiller stresses the anger Wollstonecraft revealed in her VINDICATION OF THE RIGHTS OF WOMAN and considers that this anger prevented her from writing well, although it expressed her situation as a woman. Brownmiller criticizes Wollstonecraft for insensitivity to the plight of eighteenth-century womanhood, especially when she scorns "meek" women as much as anti-feminist male writers. The Flexner biography is praised, although Brownmiller dislikes Flexner's avoidance of the "pain" of the Wollstonecraft-Imlay impasse.

370 Burwash, Ida. "Notable Marys," CANADIAN MAGAZINE OF POLITICS, SCIENCE, ART AND LITERATURE, XLVIII, November 1916 - April 1917, 236-240.

Ida Burwash sketches Wollstonecraft's life. She stresses that Wollstonecraft's importance is due to her VINDICATION OF THE RIGHTS OF WOMAN and not to her romantic life. The main arguments of THE RIGHTS OF WOMAN are summarized. Burwash refers to the hostile notices of Wollstonecraft toward the end of the eighteenth century.

371 Cameron, Kenneth Neill, ed. SHELLEY AND HIS CIRCLE:1773-
1822. Cambridge: Harvard University Press, 1961.

The manuscripts presented in this work modify some earlier
opinions about Wollstonecraft's life. For example, a bill
of exchange suggests that in 1793 Wollstonecraft was not
penniless in France and was not therefore thrown on Gilbert
Imlay for support. Several episodes in Wollstonecraft's
life are illuminated by the documents. A notable one is
the friendship between Wollstonecraft and Henry Gabell.

372 Cameron, Kenneth Neill. THE YOUNG SHELLEY: GENESIS OF A
RADICAL. New York: The Macmillan Company, 1950.

Kenneth Neill Cameron briefly sketches Wollstonecraft's
life. He discusses her possible influence on Shelley, revealed in his views on marriage, on prostitution as a social
evil, and on early childhood education. Shelley's debt to
Wollstonecraft may also be apparent in his condemnation of
capitalists as well as aristocrats and in his belief that a
dictatorial state corrupts human nature.

373 Cary, Elizabeth Luther. "John Adams and Mary Wollstonecraft,"
THE LAMP:A REVIEW OF CURRENT LITERATURE, February 1903, 35-40.

The article concerns Adams' marginal notes to Wollstonecraft's HISTORICAL AND MORAL VIEW.OF . . . THE FRENCH REVO-
LUTION. It points out several ways in which Adams' views
diverge from Wollstonecraft's.

374 Catlin, George E. G. Introduction to THE RIGHTS OF WOMAN by
Mary Wollstonecraft and THE SUBJECTION OF WOMEN by John
Stuart Mill. London: J. M. Dent, 1929.

The introduction compares and contrasts the works of Wollstonecraft and Mill; both are considered milestones marking
the advance of a great social movement. Wollstonecraft's
book is considered to be, for the purist, a bad book; it is
poorly written and planned and excessively rhetorical.
George Catlin, however, considers it redeemed by its sincerity. There is a short summary of the events of Wollstonecraft's life and a sketch of the history of attitudes toward
women. In the course of his introduction Catlin criticizes
the owners of the Wollstonecraft-Fuseli letters for their refusal to publish this correspondence.

375 CHAMBERS'S BIOGRAPHICAL DICTIONARY. New York: Macmillan Company, 1956.

The entry on Wollstonecraft briefly sketches her life, omit-
ting mention of the Fuseli episode. A VINDICATION OF THE
RIGHTS OF WOMAN is described as a work of genius which advocated the main doctrines of the modern women's movement.

376   CHAMBERS'S CYCLOPAEDIA OF ENGLISH LITERATURE. Ed. David
      Patrick. Philadelphia: J. B. Lippincott Company, 1902.

      The entry on Mary Wollstonecraft is primarily a summary of
      Wollstonecraft's life. A VINDICATION OF THE RIGHTS OF WO-
      MAN is described as a curious medley of genius and turgidity.

377   Chandler, George. WILLIAM ROSCOE OF LIVERPOOL. London:
      B. T. Batsford, 1953.

      This work publishes six letters of Wollstonecraft's, found
      in the Roscoe papers at the Liverpool City Libraries. It
      discusses the friendship between Roscoe and Wollstonecraft.

378   Chislett, William. MODERNS AND NEAR MODERNS. New York:
      Grafton Press, 1928.

      In an essay on Charles Brockden Brown and the Godwin cir-
      cle, there is some mention of Wollstonecraft and her un-
      happy relationship with Imlay.

379   CHOICE, VIII, April 1971, 224.

      In a note on Margaret George's biography, it is stated that
      the study provides no new biographical material and very
      little insight into Wollstonecraft's place in the long strug-
      gle for female emancipation.

380   CHOICE, X, May 1973, 499-500.

      In a note on Eleanor Flexner's biography of Wollstonecraft,
      it is stated that Flexner has achieved an honest and moving
      portrayal of how Wollstonecraft, the lone defender of en-
      lightenment for women, liberated herself in relation to her
      society and the obscure urges of her own psyche.

381   CHRISTIAN CENTURY, October 11, 1972, 1021.

      A note on Eleanor Flexner's biography of Wollstonecraft
      mentions that people seldom write of Wollstonecraft without
      using phrases such as "flouted convention."

382   CHRISTIAN CENTURY, January 29, 1975, 90.

      In a brief mention of Claire Tomalin's biography of Woll-
      stonecraft, it is noted that Wollstonecraft is a heroine
      to women's movements but that her life is little known.

383   Church, Richard. MARY SHELLEY. New York: The Viking Press,
      1928.

      Richard Church includes in his book a biographical sketch of
      Mary Wollstonecraft. The events of her life are placed in
      the most favorable light, and Wollstonecraft emerges as noble,

pure, rich-hearted, and impulsive. A VINDICATION OF THE
RIGHTS OF WOMAN is seen as primarily a demand that women
be regarded seriously and educated equally with men as
responsible members of society.

384   Church, Richard. SPECTATOR, August 20, 1932, 236-237.

This is a review of H. R. James's biography. It notes
Wollstonecraft's combination of courage, instinct, intellect, and passion, which gave her the power to point the
way not only toward the emancipation of women, but also
toward many other advances in social and moral growth.

385   Churchill, R. C. ENGLISH LITERATURE OF THE EIGHTEENTH
CENTURY. London: University Tutorial Press, Ltd., 1953.

Godwin's views on marriage and the family are said to have
been much modified after his experience with Wollstonecraft.

386   Clark, David Lee. "Brockden Brown and the Rights of Women,"
TEXAS UNIVERSITY BULLETIN, Comparative Literature Series,
II, 2212, March 1922, 1-48.

David Lee Clark discusses Wollstonecraft's VINDICATION OF
THE RIGHTS OF WOMAN, which he sees as unoriginal and poorly
written. He finds the book redeemed, however, by its bold-
ness, fire, and passion. Clark contends that Brockden Brown
had definite opinions on the rights of men and women before
he read Godwin and Wollstonecraft.

387   Cobb, Richard. TIMES LITERARY SUPPLEMENT, September 1974,
941-944.

Richard Cobb turns a review of Claire Tomalin's biography
of Wollstonecraft into an attack on Wollstonecraft, her
character, life, and works. He finds her silly and egotis-
tical, full of self-pity and jealousy, and her work mediocre
and ill written. He considers her life a disaster, since
she wrecked most of the people with whom she came into con-
tact. Cobb is equally scathing about Wollstonecraft's radical associates: Joseph Johnson and the "cranks" and Dissenting radicals who surrounded him. There is little about Tomalin's book in the review; Cobb finds Tomalin too indulgent
to Wollstonecraft and too generous in her assessment of her
subject's literary talents.

388   Cobban, Alfred, ed. THE DEBATE ON THE FRENCE REVOLUTION
1789-1800. London: Nicholas Kaye, 1950.

There are excerpts from Wollstonecraft's VINDICATION OF THE
RIGHTS OF MEN and A VINDICATION OF THE RIGHTS OF WOMAN.

389   Colby, Elbridge, ed. THE LIFE OF THOMAS HOLCROFT WRITTEN
BY HIMSELF CONTINUED TO THE TIME OF HIS DEATH FROM HIS DIARY

NOTES AND OTHER PAPERS BY WILLIAM HAZLITT. London: Constable & Co. Ltd., 1925.

In the introduction, Elbridge Colby mentions Wollstonecraft as a friend of Holcroft's.

390 Coleridge, Samuel Taylor. NOTEBOOKS. Ed. Kathleen Coburn. London: Routledge & Kegan Paul, 1957-1961.

Coleridge read Wollstonecraft's LETTERS WRITTEN . . . IN SWEDEN. He wrote to her "urging her to Religion."

391 Collins, John Churton. THE POSTHUMOUS ESSAYS OF COLLINS. Ed. L. C. Collins, London: J. M. Dent & Sons, 1912.

An account is given of Wollstonecraft and Godwin and their life together.

392 Colum, Mary M. "Mary Wollstonecraft," THE NATION, CXXXVI, January - June 1933, 183-185.

This is a review of H. R. James's MARY WOLLSTONECRAFT. The book is described as a very excellent account of Wollstonecraft's mind and work, although it is in no sense a biography. Mary M. Colum states that few have been more slandered than Wollstonecraft. A short account of her life and work is given. Her similarities to Burke, in spite of obvious differences of opinion, are stressed. Colum states that Wollstonecraft's contribution is not to literature or art but to political and social reform. She was a pamphleteer.

393 CONCISE UNIVERSAL BIOGRAPHY. Ed. Sir John A. Hamilton. London: Amalgamated Press, 1934.

Wollstonecraft is included.

394 Cone, C. B. AMERICAN HISTORICAL REVIEW, February 1971, 149.

In this review of Margaret George's biography of Wollstonecraft, C. B. Cone describes the book as labored and pretentious in its discussion of Wollstonecraft's childhood. It is said to be infused with righteous purpose and with Simone de Beauvoir.

395 Conrad, Barnaby. FAMOUS LAST WORDS. Garden City: Doubleday, 1968.

Wollstonecraft's last words are included.

396 Cooke, George Willis. "Woman in the Era of Revolution," THE CHAUTAUQUAN, March 1910, 19-39.

George Cooke gives a short account of Wollstonecraft. He stresses the importance of her work and the moderate and rational nature of her demands.

397   Cowie, Alexander. SATURDAY REVIEW OF LITERATURE, XVI, July
       1937, 12.

       This is a review of George Preedy's biography of Wollstone-
       craft. It criticizes the book for its cumbersome and repe-
       titious style.   /

398   Cox, Edward.Godfrey. A REFERENCE GUIDE TO THE LITERATURE
       OF TRAVEL. Seattle: University of Washington, 1935.

       Wollstonecraft's LETTERS WRITTEN . . . IN SWEDEN is listed.
       An unfavorable comment on her from the GENTLEMAN'S MAGAZINE
       of June 1836 is quoted (see 193).

399   CURRENT LITERATURE, L, January - June 1911, 633-635.

       In a review of G. R. Stirling Taylor's MARY WOLLSTONECRAFT:
       A STUDY IN ECONOMICS AND ROMANCE, entitled "The Ultra-Modern
       Teachings of Mary Wollstonecraft," there is a brief descrip-
       tion of women writers before Wollstonecraft. The importance
       of Wollstonecraft as a theorist of women's rights is stress-
       ed, as is her concern with the rights of humanity in gen-
       eral. The main arguments of Wollstonecraft's major works
       are summarized.

400   Curti, Merle. THE GROWTH OF AMERICAN THOUGHT. New York:
       Harper & Bros., 1943.

       A short section concerns the influence in America of British
       radicals, including Wollstonecraft.

401   Daiches, David. A CRITICAL HISTORY OF ENGLISH LITERATURE.
       London: Secker & Warburg, 1960.

       Wollstonecraft's VINDICATION OF THE RIGHTS OF WOMAN is con-
       sidered a significant contribution to the feminist movement
       in England.

402   Damon, S. Foster. A BLAKE DICTIONARY: THE IDEAS AND SYMBOLS
       OF WILLIAM BLAKE. Providence: Brown University Press, 1965.

       In his section on the VISIONS OF THE DAUGHTERS OF ALBION, S.
       Foster Damon states that Blake was obviously inspired by
       Wollstonecraft's VINDICATION OF THE RIGHTS OF WOMAN.

403   Damon, S. Foster. WILLIAM BLAKE: HIS PHILOSOPHY AND SYMBOLS.
       Boston: Houghton Mifflin Company, 1924.

       S. Foster Damon refers to Wollstonecraft's attempt to join
       the Fuseli household. He speculates that Wollstonecraft may
       have given Blake the idea for his poem "Mary."

404   Davis, Elizabeth Gould. THE FIRST SEX. Baltimore: Penguin
       Books, Inc. 1972.

Wollstonecraft is described as the Tom Paine of her sex.

405   Dean, Charlotte. NEW YORK TIMES BOOK REVIEW, July 11, 1937,
       6.

       In her review of George Preedy's biography of Wollstonecraft,
       Charlotte Dean gives a hostile résumé of the life. Woll-
       stonecraft is described as ambitious beyond her talents; she
       was thwarted and humiliated in love and defeated in all of
       the life that she wanted.

406   Detre, Jean. "Mary Wollstonecraft and William Godwin: A
       Revolutionary Marriage," Ms., December 1972, 78-81, 108-109.

       Jean Detre's article concerns the marriage of Wollstonecraft
       and Godwin. It also concerns the views on marriage held by
       Godwin and Wollstonecraft before 1797. Detre notes Godwin's
       prejudices against women, revealed in his association of men
       with logic and women with feeling, but she stresses
       Godwin's courage in fighting against external prejudices
       that surround women. In her article Detre quotes liberally
       from the letters of Godwin and Wollstonecraft.

407   Detre, Jean. A MOST EXTRAORDINARY PAIR: MARY WOLLSTONECRAFT
       AND WILLIAM GODWIN. New York: Doubleday, 1975.

       The book includes the letters of Wollstonecraft and Godwin
       written during 1796 and 1797. They are supplemented by a
       fictional journal written by Jean Detre to express what she
       believes would have been Wollstonecraft's feelings during
       the period of her relationship with Godwin. Much attention
       is given to the problem of marriage.

408   Dorland, W. A. Newman. THE SUM OF FEMININE ACHIEVEMENT: A
       CRITICAL AND ANALYTICAL STUDY OF WOMAN'S CONTRIBUTION TO THE
       INTELLECTUAL PROGRESS OF THE WORLD. Boston: The Stratford
       Company, 1917.

       Wollstonecraft is included in the study. She is described
       as the great pioneer of the woman's movement.

409   Douglass, Emily Taft. REMEMBER THE LADIES: THE STORY OF
       GREAT WOMEN WHO HELPED SHAPE AMERICA. New York: G. P. Put-
       nam's Sons, 1966.

       Wollstonecraft is described as a high-strung former gover-
       ness. The main arguments of A VINDICATION OF THE RIGHTS OF
       WOMAN are briefly summarized. Fanny Wright is described as
       Wollstonecraft's spiritual daughter.

410   Dolleans, Edouard. DRAMES INTERIEURS. Paris, 1944.

       There is a section on Wollstonecraft and Godwin and on their
       marriage, which is seen as a contradiction of Godwin's theo-
       ries.

411 Downs, Robert B. MOLDERS OF THE MODERN MIND: THREE BOOKS
THAT SHAPED WESTERN CIVILIZATION. New York: Barnes and
Noble, 1961.

Wollstonecraft's VINDICATION OF THE RIGHTS OF WOMAN is
included.

412 Drabble, Margaret. "Mary, Quite Contrary," THE SPECTATOR,
September 14, 1974, 338-339.

In her review of Claire Tomalin's biography, Margaret Drabble provides a sympathetic sketch of Wollstonecraft's life.

413 Dunlap, William. DIARY; THE MEMOIRS OF A DRAMATIST, THEAT-
RICAL MANAGER, PAINTER, CRITIC, NOVELIST, AND HISTORIAN.
New York: John Watts DePeyster Publication Fund, 1931.

Wollstonecraft's life with Godwin and her death are described.

414 Durant, W. Clark. NOTES AND QUERIES, Series 12, IX, December 17, 1921, 490.

This is a query about the exact nature of an act of misconduct attributed to a Kingsborough daughter. The misconduct
was mentioned in a scurrilous review of A VINDICATION OF THE
RIGHTS OF WOMAN as an example of Wollstonecraft's influence
on her charges.

415 Durant, W. Clark. NOTES AND QUERIES, Series 13, XIII, July
7, 1923, 11-12.

W. Clark Durant emends the date of a letter by Wollstonecraft and points out the faulty chronology in Kegan Paul's
biography in the light of Godwin's MEMOIRS and Wollstonecraft's own writings.

416 Durant, W. Clark. "Mary Wollstonecraft," TIMES LITERARY
SUPPLEMENT, June 28, 1923, 440.

W. Clark Durant mentions Wollstonecraft's still unpublished
papers.

417 Durant, W. Clark. Preface and Supplement to MEMOIRS OF
MARY WOLLSTONECRAFT. London: Constable & Co., Ltd., 1927.

In his Preface, W. Clark Durant summarizes the criticism on
Wollstonecraft. He tries to establish her connection with
Blake, whose poem, "Mary," Durant believes she inspired.
He stresses Wollstonecraft's mystical nature, akin to Blake's.
In his Supplement, Durant adds many facts to Godwin's account,
and he uses Wollstonecraft's novels to throw light on her
life. In his biographical summary, Durant includes many let-
ters of Wollstonecraft to Joseph Johnson, written while she

was in Ireland, and others to friends and relations. He traces the history of several collections of Wollstonecraft letters, especially those to Miss Massey and those to Fuseli, apparently lost by the Shelley family.

418 Dysin, H.V.D. and John Butt. "Augustans and Romantics," INTRODUCTION TO ENGLISH LITERATURE. Ed. Bonamy Dobree. 1940; London: Cresset Press, 1958.

Wollstonecraft and her works are briefly discussed.

419 Earland, Ada. JOHN OPIE AND HIS CIRCLE. London: Hutchinson & Co., 1911.

Wollstonecraft's relationships with Opie and Amelia Alderson are mentioned.

420 EDINBURGH REVIEW OR CRITICAL JOURNAL, CCXI, 1910, 306-323.

This is a review of Emma Rauschenbusch-Clough's STUDY OF MARY WOLLSTONECRAFT AND THE RIGHTS OF WOMAN, the Fawcett and Pennell editions of A VINDICATION OF THE RIGHTS OF WOMAN and the Kegan Paul and Ingpen editions of the LETTERS TO IMLAY. The review makes general remarks on intellectual women in general and on the lot of women in the eighteenth century in particular. A fairly full account of Wollstonecraft's life is given with quotations from her works. Her love of adventure and her curiosity are stressed.

421. Eliot, George. THE GEORGE ELIOT LETTERS. Ed. Gordon S. Haight. New Haven: Yale University Press, 1955.

In a letter written in 1871, George Eliot compares her depression to that of Wollstonecraft. She expresses her satisfaction that she did not, like Wollstonecraft, attempt suicide.

422 Eliot, George. "Margaret Fuller and Mary Wollstonecraft," ESSAYS OF GEORGE ELIOT. Ed. Thomas Pinney. London: Routledge; New York: Columbia University Press, 1963.

This is a reprinting of the essay first published in the LEADER in 1855. (see 181).

423 Elton, Oliver. A SURVEY OF ENGLISH LITERATURE 1780-1830. New York: Longmans, Green, and Co., 1912.

In a section on the prose of doctrine, Mary Wollstonecraft's VINDICATION OF THE RIGHTS OF WOMAN is briefly mentioned. It is compared with Godwin's POLITICAL JUSTICE and is found to be superior in good sense and sound prophecy, although its style is considered rambling and turgid. Elton says that Wollstonecraft cannot write but that she is all the more eloquent because of this. THE RIGHTS OF WOMAN is seen as marred by an inexperience of passion. The rights vindicated are moderate and are not primarily legal and political. Wollstonecraft wants women to be like men only in reason and comprehension of duty.

424 Elsner, Paul. PERCY BYSSHE SHELLYS ABHANGIGKEIT VON WILLIAM GODWINS POLITICAL JUSTICE. Berlin, 1906.

The influence of Wollstonecraft on Shelley is briefly mentioned.

425 Emerson, Oliver Farrar. "Notes on Gilbert Imlay, Early American Writer," PMLA, XXXIX, June 1924, 406-439.

Oliver Emerson makes two observations on Wollstonecraft: first, that she met in Hamburg the French-American, Crevecoeur, who may have influenced the writings of Gilbert Imlay; second, that her VINDICATION OF THE RIGHTS OF WOMAN may have influenced Imlay's book, THE EMIGRANTS.

426 ENCYCLOPEDIA AMERICANA. New York, 1963.

The entry on Wollstonecraft is a much shortened version of Arthur Nason's entry in the 1943 edition (see 545).

427 ENCYCLOPEDIA BRITANNICA, 1910.

The entry on Wollstonecraft consists of a brief biography and description of her works. It states that it is the language rather than the content of A VINDICATION OF THE RIGHTS OF WOMAN that caused the outcry. It is pointed out that Wollstonecraft opposed Rousseau's attitudes toward women, although she was in other respects his disciple.

428 ENCLYCLOPEDIA BRITANNICA, 1968.

The entry on Wollstonecraft inaccurately describes her life and works. Personal loyalty to Tom Paine is said to have prompted her VINDICATION OF THE RIGHTS OF MEN, whose date is given as 1793. Wollstonecraft is called a miscellaneous writer and a passionate advocate of women's equality.

429 THE ENCYCLOPEDIA AND DICTIONARY OF EDUCATION. Ed. Foster Watson. London: Sir Isaac Pitman & Sons, Ltd., 1921.

Though somewhat critical of Wollstonecraft's psychology in A VINDICATION OF THE RIGHTS OF WOMAN, this biographical sketch acknowledges its importance as a document in the history of women's education. Wollstonecraft's ideas are said to have been far in advance of their time.

430 England, Martha Winburn. "Two Great Lives, and One Lesser

Life," WOMEN'S STUDIES, II, I, 127-31.

This is a review of three biographies, one of which is Eleanor Flexner's MARY WOLLSTONECRAFT, A BIOGRAPHY.

431 Erdman, David. BLAKE; PROPHET AGAINST EMPIRE. Princeton: Princeton University Press, 1954.

David Erdman considers that Blake probably read Wollstone-craft's VINDICATION OF THE RIGHTS OF MEN and her VINDICA-TION OF THE RIGHTS OF WOMAN. He relates Blake's VISIONS OF THE DAUGHTERS OF ALBION to the two VINDICATIONS. He states that a knowledge of Wollstonecraft's idea, expressed in THE RIGHTS OF MEN, that the large estates should be divided into small farms, helps the reader to understand the more elliptical economic observations of Oothoon. He finds Woll-stonecraft's peasant-proprietor ideal relevant to Blake's thinking, and he notes the similarity between Blake's and Wollstonecraft's stand on enclosure.

432 Ernle, Rowland E. P. THE LIGHT READING OF OUR ANCESTORS. 1927; New York: Books for Libraries Press, 1970.

Wollstonecraft is mentioned as the original of Henrietta in MANDEVILLE and of Marguerite in ST. LEON.

433 Faehler, Karl. "Studien zum Lebensbild eines Deutschen Weltburgers, des Grafen von Schlabrendorf." Dissertation. Munich, 1909.

This study mentions Wollstonecraft's relationship with Von Schlabrendorf and quotes from her letter to him.

434 Fairchild, Hoxie Neale. THE NOBLE SAVAGE: A STUDY IN RO-MANTIC NATURALISM. New York: Columbia University Press, 1928.

The book has some discussion of Wollstonecraft's HISTORICAL AND MORAL VIEW OF THE ORIGIN AND PROGRESS OF THE FRENCH REVOLUTION. It describes Wollstonecraft as a perfectibili-tarian who hails the revolution as the embodiment of the lofty doctrines of the philosophes.

435 Farington, Joseph. THE FARINGTON DIARY. Ed. James Greig. London: Hutchinson & Co., 1923.

There is a contemporary account of Wollstonecraft's attemp-ted suicide at Putney; in it she is referred to as Mrs. Im-lay.

436 Fauchery, Pierre. LA DESTINEE FEMININE DANS LE ROMAN EURO-PEEN DU DIX-HUITIEME SIECLE 1713-1807. Paris: Librairie Armand Colin, 1972.

Pierre Fauchery mentions Wollstonecraft in passing. He
refers to the autobiographical nature of MARY, A FICTION
and to the suggestion of sexual rights for women in THE
WRONGS OF WOMAN.

437 Fawcett, Millicent Garrett. "A Pioneer of the Movement,"
THE CASE FOR WOMEN'S SUFFRAGE. Ed. Brougham Villiers
(Frederick John Shaw). London: T. Fisher Unwin, 1907.

The essay on Wollstonecraft describes her as the product as
well as the earliest confessor of the women's rights movement. She is said to have proved the falsity of the notion
that makes the place of women entirely dependent on their
usefulness and ageeableness to men, while she retained a
keen appreciation of the sanctity of women's domestic duties and their importance to the individual, the family,
and the state. Millicent Fawcett summarizes and comments
on some of the main arguments of A VINDICATION OF THE RIGHTS
OF WOMAN. The lack of organization and order of the book
may, in Fawcett's view, be the result of Wollstonecraft's
defective education.

438 Fawcett, Millicent Garrett. WOMEN'S SUFFRAGE: A SHORT HIS-
TORY OF A GREAT MOVEMENT. 1912; New York: Source Book Press,
1970.

On her first page, Millicent Fawcett refers to Mary Wollstonecraft who is described as starting the demand of women
for political liberty in England. Fawcett asserts that the
torch lighted by Wollstonecraft was never afterwards extin-
guished.

439 Fennessy, R. R. BURKE, PAINE, AND THE RIGHTS OF MAN. The
Hague: Martinus Nijhoff, 1963.

R. R. Fennessy deals briefly with Mary Wollstonecraft's
VINDICATION OF THE RIGHTS OF MEN. He describes her attack
on Burke as direct and personal. The main ideas of THE
RIGHTS OF MEN are summarized, and special emphasis is given
to Wollstonecraft's condemnation of property and her attack
on the established church.

440 Ferguson, Moira Campbell. "Declarations of Independence:
The Rebel Heroine, 1684-1800." Dissertation. Washington,
1973.

The dissertation includes a section on the novels of Mary
Wollstonecraft.

441 Ferguson, Moira. Introduction to MARIA; OR THE WRONGS OF
WOMAN by Mary Wollstonecraft. New York: Norton, 1975.

The introduction concerns Wollstonecraft and her pivotal
position in the history of humanist and particularly femin-

ist thought. It retells the story of her life and relates it to THE WRONGS OF WOMAN. The book itself is seen as the first novelistic attempt in the language to depict female degradation with grim realism. This it does through Maria, who suffers from the evils of marriage and the marriage laws, and through Jemima, who suffers every imaginable agony and humiliation possible to women.

442 Flanders, W. A. "The Didactic and 'Philosophical' Novel in England, 1792-1805." Dissertation. Wisconsin, 1964.

W. A. Flanders discusses the content and style of representative novels of social and political commentary and controversy from 1792 to 1805, and relates them to the tradition of the English novel as it stood at the time. Mary Wollstonecraft's WRONG OF WOMAN; OR MARIA is discussed among the novels of the liberal woman writers such as Smith, Inchbald, and Hays.

443 Fleisher, David. WILLIAM GODWIN: A STUDY IN LIBERALISM. London: George Allen & Unwin, 1951.

Wollstonecraft's life with Godwin is described and her effect on him discussed. She is seen as giving him an appreciation of the forces of emotion and imagination. The MEMOIRS is considered an honest book.

444 Flexner, Eleanor. MARY WOLLSTONECRAFT: A BIOGRAPHY. New York: Coward, McCann and Geoghegan, 1972.

Eleanor Flexner relates the events of Wollstonecraft's life. She claims to emphasize the life rather than the intellectual trends in the formation of Wollstonecraft's ideas. The early years are treated in detail and the emotional patterns created during this time are discussed and illustrated. Flexner emphasizes several qualities in Wollstonecraft. One is her piety, already noted by C. Kegan Paul (see 264). Another is her insensitivity to the feelings of other women. Flexner is especially critical of her treatment of her sisters. Flexner's biography is based on previous biographies supplemented by much original material. Several of Wollstonecraft's letters are published here for the first time. There are several appendices. The first concerns Edward Wollstonecraft's property and will; the second discusses the possible love affair between Mary Wollstonecraft and Joshua Waterhouse (see also 555 and 677). The third appendix outlines the relationship of "Mrs Mason," Margaret King, and Wollstonecraft's daughter, Mary Shelley; the fourth considers the authorship of the reviews in the ANALYTICAL REVIEW. Flexner expresses her disagreement with Wardle and with Derek Roper (see 594 and 676). There is a bibliographical summary and copious notes to the text, but no bibliography.

445   Foster, James R. HISTORY OF THE PRE-ROMANTIC NOVEL IN ENG-
      LAND. New York: MLA, 1949.

      James Foster briefly discusses Wollstonecraft's novels. He
      describes MARY, A FICTION as rough and unfinished, yet in-
      teresting because it attempts to trace the intellectual and
      moral development of a new woman. THE WRONGS OF WOMAN is
      described as based on Wollstonecraft's own wrongs and those
      of other women.

446   Frankau, Pamela. Introduction to THE RIGHTS OF WOMAN and
      THE SUBJECTION OF WOMEN. London: J. M. Dent & Sons Ltd.,
      1955.

      Pamel Frankau states that Wollstonecraft's VINDICATION OF
      THE RIGHTS OF WOMAN and J. S. Mill's THE SUBJECTION OF WO-
      MEN belong together and that they complement each other
      perfectly. THE RIGHTS OF WOMAN is described as a stimula-
      ting and an exasperating work. Through it, Wollstonecraft's
      ungovernable personality emerges. Frankau considers that
      Wollstonecraft's battle is still going on, since the inflex-
      ibility of the human mind towards women remains.

447   FREEDOM, XXII, July 1908, 50.

      In a review of Victor Robinson's WILLIAM GODWIN AND MARY
      WOLLSTONECRAFT, there is praise of Wollstonecraft and of
      her VINDICATION OF THE RIGHTS OF WOMAN.

448   Friedan, Betty. THE FEMININE MYSTIQUE. New York: W. W.
      Norton, 1963.

      There are brief mentions of Wollstonecraft. She is des-
      cribed as spearheading the feminist movement in England.

449   Fuller, Edmund. "Two Feminists Of Times Past," WALL STREET
      JOURNAL, June 5, 1973, 22.

      This is a review of Eleanor Flexner's biography of Woll-
      stonecraft and of Noel B. Gerson's DAUGHTER OF EARTH AND
      WATER: A BIOGRAPHY OF MARY WOLLSTONECRAFT SHELLEY. Ed-
      mund Fuller states that, reading the two books together,
      one feels the deprivation of both women of not knowing
      each other.

450   Gardner, Charles. WILLIAM BLAKE THE MAN. London: J. M.
      Dent & Sons, Ltd., 1919.

      Charles Gardner stresses the independence of Wollstone-
      craft's thinking and the loneliness of her life. He points
      out the similarities between Blake and Wollstonecraft and
      considers that, had Blake been single and she drawn into
      friendship with him, she would have become the perfect type
      of the new woman.

451 Garnett, Richard. ATHENAEUM, 3955, August 15, 1903, 219.

In a note, Richard Garnett expresses ignorance of the fate
of Gilbert Imlay. With reference to Imlay, he quotes the
lines on the "base Indian."

452 Gattey, Charles Neilson. GAUGIN'S ASTONISHING GRANDMOTHER.
London: Femina Books Ltd., 1970.

Flora Tristan is said to have greatly admired Wollstonecraft
and to have wholeheartedly approved of the contents of A
VINDICATION OF THE RIGHTS OF WOMAN.

453 Gaunt, William. ARROWS OF DESIRE: A STUDY OF WILLIAM
BLAKE AND HIS ROMANTIC WORLD. London: Museum Press, 1956.

William Gaunt sees Mary Wollstonecraft as the ideal woman
of Fuseli, Blake, and Lavater. He gives a summary of her
life to prove her fitness for this role. He considers that
Blake might have had Wollstonecraft in mind when he wrote
his poem "Mary."

454 Gerson, Noel.B. DAUGHTER OF EARTH AND WATER: A BIOGRAPHY
OF MARY WOLLSTONECRAFT SHELLEY. New York: William Morrow &
Company Inc., 1973.

Wollstonecraft's life is summarized and the arguments of A
VINDICATION OF THE RIGHTS OF WOMAN briefly sketched. Wollstonecraft is described as perhaps the most intelligent woman of her day. Noel Gerson mentions Mary Shelley's resemblance to her mother. This resemblance attracted Shelley
to her. There is a description of Mary Shelley's visits to
her mother's grave.

455 Gooch, G. P. "Europe and the French Revolution," CAMBRIDGE
MODERN HISTORY. London: Macmillan & Co., Ltd., 1904.

Wollstonecraft is said to have boldly declared sex to be a
secondary consideration and to have demanded that men and
women meet on the ground of their common humanity.

456 Goodwin, June. CHRISTIAN SCIENCE MONITOR, February 7, 1975,
10.

In her review of Claire Tomalin's biography of Wollstonecraft, June Goodwin describes Wollstonecraft as a woman of
all kinds of intelligence and all kinds of aggravating
traits.

457 Gorman, Herbert. NEW YORK TIMES, July 24, 1927, 11.

In his review of Durant's edition of Godwin's MEMOIRS, Herbert Gorman refers to the hostile reaction of the public to
the work. There is a summary of Wollstonecraft's life.

458   Goulianos, Joan, ed. BY A WOMAN WRITT: LITERATURE FROM SIX
      CENTURIES BY AND ABOUT WOMEN. Baltimore: Penguin, 1974.

      In her anthology, Joan Goulianos includes a selection from
      Mary Wollstonecraft's work, A VINDICATION OF THE RIGHTS
      OF WOMAN and from the LETTERS TO IMLAY. The short introduc-
      tion to Wollstonecraft calls THE RIGHTS OF WOMAN a reasoned
      and passionate appeal for women's independence and states
      that the LETTERS TO IMLAY suggest the extent of Wollstone-
      craft's subjection to women's oppression.

459   Gourg, Raymond. WILLIAM GODWIN (1756-1836). Paris: Felix
      Alcan, 1908.

      A short biographical sketch of Wollstonecraft is given.

460   Grabo, Carl. THE MAGIC PLANT: THE GROWTH OF SHELLEY'S
      THOUGHT. Chapel Hill: University of North Carolina Press,
      1936.

      Wollstonecraft is mentioned as an influence on Shelley.
      There is a summary of her theory of economic equality, ex-
      pressed in her work on the French Revolution.

461   Greer, Germaine. THE FEMALE EUNUCH. New York: McGraw-Hill
      Book Company, 1971.

      Several quotations from A VINDICATION OF THE RIGHTS OF WO-
      MAN are included in the book.

462   Gregory, Allene. THE FRENCH REVOLUTION AND THE ENGLISH NO-
      VEL. New York: G. P. Putnam's Sons, 1915.

      Allene Gregory includes in her book a section on Mary Woll-
      stonecraft. It deals briefly with A VINDICATION OF THE
      RIGHTS OF WOMAN, which is seen as a surprisingly modern de-
      mand for a sound education.and the right to work. The nov-
      els are described as a very insignificant part of Wollstone-
      craft's literary output. Gregory summarizes Wollstonecraft's
      life and provides the plots of the three novels, MARY, A FIC-
      TION, THE WRONGS OF WOMAN: OR MARIA, and THE CAVE OF FANCY.

463   Gregory, Horace. "A Feminist Rousseau," NEW YORK HERALD TRI-
      BUNE BOOKS, October 30, 1932, 15.

      In his review of H. R. James's biography of Wollstonecraft,
      Horace Gregory states that, from the publication of A VINDI-
      CATION OF THE RIGHTS OF WOMAN, the feminist movement for
      equal suffrage took coherent form. Wollstonecraft is des-
      cribed as the English version of Rousseau and she is consid-
      ered important as a thinker and pioneer. James's biography
      is criticized for its melodramatic treatment of Wollstone-
      craft.

464 Grylls, Rosalie Glynn. "Mary Wollstonecraft and After, 1759-1959, A Bi-Centenary Tribute," CHARLES LAMB SOCIETY BULLETIN, CXLVIII, May 1959, 239-240.

This is a short sketch of Wollstonecraft's life; her importance is noted.

465 Grylls, Rosalie Glynn. WILLIAM GODWIN AND HIS WORLD. London: Odhams Press, 1953.

Rosalie Grylls summarizes the events of Wollstonecraft's life. She stresses that, as a woman, Wollstonecraft was not at all the emancipated female of the lampoons, and was in reality dependent and vulnerable. A VINDICATION OF THE RIGHTS OF WOMAN is regarded not as a feminist manifesto but as a call to duties.

466 Hagelman, Charles W. A VINDICATION OF THE RIGHTS OF WOMAN by Mary Wollstonecraft. New York: Norton, 1967.

In his introduction, Charles Hagelman considers that, in a general sense, the greater part of Wollstonecraft's life was a preparation for the writing of THE RIGHTS OF WOMAN, but, in a restricted sense, its writing began with A VINDICATION OF THE RIGHTS OF MEN. Much of the introduction concerns THE RIGHTS OF MEN and the controversy that gave rise to it, for Hagelman sees THE RIGHTS OF MEN as historically and thematically an introduction to THE RIGHTS OF WOMAN. Hagelman finds Wollstonecraft's timeless appeal not primarily in the originality or the profundity of her ideas, nor in the eloquence of her prose, but in her devotion to her fellow men and her concern for their well being.

467 Halévy, Elie. THE GROWTH OF PHILOSOPHIC RADICALISM. Boston: Beacon Press, 1955.

Elie Halévy mentions Wollstonecraft, but does not treat her in detail.

468 Hall, Walter P. BRITISH RADICALISM 1791-1797. New York: Columbia University, 1912.

A VINDICATION OF THE RIGHTS OF MEN is discussed among other works attacking Burke's REFLECTIONS. Wollstonecraft's life is briefly sketched.

469 Haller, William. THE EARLY LIFE OF ROBERT SOUTHEY, 1744-1803. New York: Columbia University, 1917.

Southey's meetings with Wollstonecraft are described.

470 Hamilton, C. J. "The Romance of A Strong Minded Woman," WESTMINSTER REVIEW, CLXXIV, July - December 1910, 176-186.

C. J. Hamilton describes Wollstonecraft as one of the most notable and pathetic figures that the latter part of the eighteenth century produced. He considers her most obvious quality her openness, and he praises her strong brain and warm heart. He gives a brief sketch of her life, the facts taken primarily from Kegan Paul.

471 Hardt, Ulrich Hermann. "A Critical Edition of Mary Wollstonecraft's A VINDICATION OF THE RIGHTS OF WOMAN: WITH STRICTURES ON POLITICAL AND MORAL SUBJECTS." Dissertation. Oregon, 1974.

Ulrich Hardt states that he has recovered as completely as possible the author's intentions as represented in the editions of A VINDICATION OF THE RIGHTS OF WOMAN over which she had some control. He records all differences between the first and second editions of 1792. To gain a critical text, he has collated five editions. The textual introduction explains the textual method of the editor and its rationale. It includes a discussion of principal editions, and of the direction of authorial emendation.

472 Hare, Robert R. "Charles Brockden Brown's ORMOND: the influence of Rousseau, Godwin and Mary Wollstonecraft." Dissertation. Maryland, 1968.

Robert R. Hare states that Brown was interested in Mary Wollstonecraft's theories, but saw a conflict in her marriage to Godwin. ORMOND grew out of his reading of Godwin's MEMOIRS OF THE AUTHOR OF A VINDICATION OF THE RIGHTS OF WOMAN. It dramatizes the conflicts between Rousseauistic, Wollstonecraftian, and Godwinian ideas on education, love, and marriage. The four female characters in ORMOND represent the four faces of Wollstonecraft.

473 Hare, Robert R. "The Base Indian: A Vindication of the Rights of Mary Wollstonecraft," MA thesis. Delaware, 1957.

Robert R. Hare argues that Mary Wollstonecraft, not Gilbert Imlay, is the author of THE EMIGRANTS and A TOPOLOGICAL DESCRIPTION OF THE WESTERN TERRITORY OF NORTH AMERICA. THE EMIGRANTS deals with material intended by Wollstonecraft for a sequel to A VINDICATION OF THE RIGHTS OF WOMAN, and there is close similarity between THE EMIGRANTS and THE WRONGS OF WOMAN. THE EMIGRANTS and A TOPOLOGICAL DESCRIPTION are consistent in style, opinion, and attitude with Wollstonecraft's works.

474 Hayden, Lucy Kelley. "A Rhetorical Analysis of Mary Wollstonecraft's A VINDICATION OF THE RIGHTS OF WOMAN." Dissertation. Michigan, 1971.

Lucy Hayden aims to reveal Wollstonecraft's major ideas concerning morals and education, to analyze the rhetorical method used to persuade the audience to accept the ideas, and to evaluate the effect of the rhetorical powers on the audience. Hayden discusses Wollstonecraft's moral theory that bases virtue on understanding and reason, and her educational theory that aims at the training of women for moral responsibilities. According to Hayden, Wollstonecraft uses rhetorical strategies and ordering devices, and she demonstrates some knowledge of audience psychology by her appeals to common consent, logic and emotions. The tone of THE RIGHTS OF WOMAN is said to vary from violent diatribe to controlled reasoning. Hayden states that Wollstonecraft is always sincere, benevolent, and determined.

475 Hazlitt,William. WORKS OF WILLIAM HAZLITT. Ed. P. P. Howe. London: J. M. Dent & Sons, 1930-34.

Hazlitt considers unfair Coleridge's statement concerning the superiority of people of imagination over people of understanding, exemplified in the superiority of Wollstonecraft over Godwin.

476 Hearn, Lafcadio. INTERPRETATIONS OF LITERATURE. Ed. John Erskine. London: William Heinemann, 1916.

There is some comment on Wollstonecraft and her relationship with Godwin.

477 Hearn, Lafcadio. A HISTORY OF ENGLISH LITERATURE IN A SERIES OF LECTURES. Tokyo: Hokuseido Press, 1927.

Wollstonecraft is discussed among other revolutionary writers.

478 Hilbish, Florence May Anna. "Charlotte Smith, Poet and Novelist (1749-1806)." Dissertation. Pennsylvania, 1941.

Wollstonecraft is mentioned in a discussion of the preface to Charlotte Smith's YOUNG PHILOSOPHER. Florence Hilbish states that Smith did not read THE WRONGS OF WOMAN early enough to show its influence in her own work. Smith's attitude to marriage is said to resemble Wollstonecraft's, although she is not as radical as Wollstonecraft in her demand for women's rights. Hilbish considers that Smith was not influenced by Wollstonecraft's VINDICATION OF THE RIGHTS OF WOMAN but that Wollstonecraft may have been influenced by Smith when she echoed in her work on the French Revolution the sentiments concerning the chaos of France expressed earlier in Smith's novel DESMOND.

479 Hobman, D. L. GO SPIN,YOU JADE! London: Watts, 1957.

D. L. Hobman includes in this book a summary of Wollstonecraft's life. A VINDICATION OF THE RIGHTS OF WOMAN is discussed and its modernity noted, especially in its pleas for coeducation and for physical exercise and a broad curriculum for girls. Hobman states that Wollstonecraft exalted happy family life and motherhood but pleaded too for the unmarried.

480 Holcroft, Thomas. THE LIFE OF THOMAS HOLCROFT WRITTEN BY HIMSELF CONTINUED TO THE TIME OF HIS DEATH FROM HIS DIARY NOTES AND OTHER PAPERS BY WILLIAM HAZLITT. Ed. Elbridge Colby. London: Constable & Company Ltd., 1925.

A letter of Holcroft dated July 1797 is addressed to both Wollstonecraft and Godwin.

481 Holtby, Winifred. WOMEN AND A CHANGING CIVILISATION. London: John Lane, 1934.

There is a section in the book entitled "The importance of Mary Wollstonecraft." The importance is seen to lie in Wollstonecraft's genius for indiscretion during an age when a woman's first duty was to be discreet. A VINDICATION OF THE RIGHTS OF WOMAN is described as a bad book, straggling and uneven, but nonetheless great in its vision and passion.

482 Hopkins, Mary Alden. HANNAH MORE AND HER CIRCLE. New York: Longmans, Green and Co., 1947.

There is mention of Hannah More's refusal to read Wollstonecraft's VINDICATION OF THE RIGHTS OF WOMAN.

483 Horner, Joyce M. THE ENGLISH WOMEN NOVELISTS AND THEIR CONNECTION WITH THE FEMINIST MOVEMENT (1688-1797). Smith College Studies in Modern Languages, XI, 1930.

Joyce Horner states that Wollstonecraft was a controversialist anxious to make as much of her case as possible, and that she claimed more for her sex than the majority would have wished to claim. Wollstonecraft's attack is considered unnecessarily violent, considering the society in which she lived.

484 Howe, P. P. THE LIFE OF WILLIAM HAZLITT. London: Hamish Hamilton, 1947.

There is reference to Hazlitt's impression of Wollstonecraft; he noted how easily she countered Godwin's arguments. Hazlitt's description of Wollstonecraft led to Coleridge's remarks contrasting people of imagination with people of intellect. Coleridge is said to have admired Wollstonecraft's conversation but not her books.

485 Howe, Will D. CHARLES LAMB AND HIS FRIENDS. Indianapolis: Bobbs-Merrill Co., 1944.

Wollstonecraft is briefly discussed in a section primarily about William Godwin.

486 Hubbard, Alice. LIFE LESSONS; TRUTHS CONCERNING PEOPLE WHO HAVE LIVED . . . FOR THE YOUNG OF ALL AGES. New York: The Roycrofters, 1909.

There is an enthusiastic sketch of the life of Mary Wollstonecraft. She is frequently described as an idealist.

487 INDEPENDENT, March 30, 1911, 668.

This is a review of G. R. Stirling Taylor's biography of Wollstonecraft. It finds much to praise in the work but blames it for its lack of literary vigor.

488 Ingpen, Roger. THE LOVE LETTERS OF MARY WOLLSTONECRAFT TO GILBERT IMLAY, with a prefatory memoir. London: Hutchinson & Co., 1908.

The memoir recounts in some detail the events of Wollstonecraft's life, relying heavily on the facts established by C. Kegan Paul. Ingpen finds the MEMOIRS of Wollstonecraft by Godwin beautiful but detrimental to her reputation, for it was the partial cause of the stigma attached to her name for two generations. C. Kegan Paul's treatment of Wollstonecraft is credited with evoking sympathy for her at a time when her books were no longer read. Ingpen describes A VINDICATION OF THE RIGHTS OF WOMAN as a strikingly original but most unequal book, and he sees it primarily as a plea for a more enlightened system of education. In his view the book contains too much theory and so is obsolete to a great extent. It is linked with the French Revolution and with French ideas.

489 Ingpen, Roger. "Mary Wollstonecraft: A Letter and Some Notes," BOOKMAN, XLIV, 1913, 164-166.

The letter of Wollstonecraft which Roger Ingpen gives in his article concerns THE WRONGS OF WOMAN and remarks made on it by George Dyson. Ingpen gives a short description of the novel and states that it was based on the events in the life of Wollstonecraft's sister, Mrs. Bishop. The remainder of the article concerns Wollstonecraft's tomb in St. Pancras and the removal of her body to Bournemouth.

490 Ishill, Joseph, ed. FREE VISTAS: AN ANTHOLOGY OF LIFE AND LETTERS. Berkeley Heights, New Jersey: Published privately at the Oriole Press, 1933.

In a letter to Joseph Ishill, Emma Goldman praises Godwin's acceptance of Wollstonecraft in spite of her illegitimate child.

491   James, H. R. MARY WOLLSTONECRAFT: A SKETCH. London: Oxford
      University Press, 1932.

      In his Preface, H. R. James connects Mary Wollstonecraft to
      the later women's suffrage movement; she is the first to
      dream of women's representation in Parliament. James's book
      was written in 1928 when, as a note states, Wollstonecraft's
      dream was receiving its logical fulfillment in the Franchise
      Act. James's aim in his sketch is to bring out the particu-
      lar apprehensions of Wollstonecraft's life and character
      which seemed to him to agree best with the records remaining.
      His interest appears to have centered on her character rather
      than her works for he believed that she was herself greater
      than her works. These works are discussed primarily for
      their revelation of her character.

492   Jebb, Camilla. MARY WOLLSTONECRAFT. London: Herbert &
      Daniel, 1912.

      The book is primarily a selection of extracts from Woll-
      stonecraft's works: A VINDICATION OF THE RIGHTS OF MEN, A
      VINDICATION OF THE RIGHTS OF WOMEN, AN HISTORICAL AND MORAL
      VIEW OF THE . . . FRENCH REVOLUTION, LETTERS WRITTEN . . .
      IN SWEDEN, personal letters, MARY, A FICTION, THE WRONGS OF
      WOMAN, and Lessons from the POSTHUMOUS WORKS. There is a
      lengthy introduction which relates the events of Wollstone-
      craft's life and considers her literary works. Wollstone-
      craft is judged to be a woman singularly original in thought
      and noble in character. The merits of her works are consid-
      ered her own, while the defects are those of her age. Ca-
      milla Jebb argues that THE RIGHTS OF WOMAN, although it has
      many grave faults of method and style, is yet a work of
      great power and originality. At the end of her book of se-
      lections, Jebb quotes several opinions of early writers on
      Wollstonecraft.

493   Jensen, Oliver. THE REVOLT OF AMERICAN WOMEN. New York:
      Harcourt, Brace & Co., 1952.

      In a short biographical sketch, Wollstonecraft is character-
      ized as an extreme neurotic and a man-hater, whose VINDICA-
      TION OF THE RIGHTS OF WOMAN served as gospel to later femin-
      ists, particularly Margaret Fuller.

494   Johnson, Diane. "Mary, Mary Quite Contrary," BOOK WORLD,
      VII, October 8, 1972, 1-2.

      In her review of Eleanor Flexner's biography of Wollstone-
      craft, Diane Johnson describes A VINDICATION OF THE RIGHTS
      OF WOMAN as an eloquent and passionate work, which derived
      its force from the circumstances of its author's life. In
      Johnson's view, Flexner's biography reveals Wollstonecraft
      to be far from the obsessive feminist she is sometimes made
      out to be. She was troubled by the same biological and in-
      tellectual role conflicts that still trouble women today.

495 Jones, Frederick L., ed. THE LETTERS OF MARY SHELLEY. Norman: University of Oklahoma Press, 1944.

In Appendix II, entitled "Mary Shelley, John Howard Payne and Washington Irving," Frederick Jones compares and contrasts the characters of Wollstonecraft and Mary Shelley. He states that both were given to melancholia, but that the quality in Wollstonecraft was partially offset by strength of character and forcefulness of personality, lacking in her daughter. Although preferring the support of a stronger person, Wollstonecraft could stand alone; Mary Shelley found such independence more difficult.

496 Jones, Frederick L. "Mary Shelley to Maria Gisborne; New Letters, 1818-1822." STUDIES IN PHILOLOGY, LII, 1955.

In a footnote, Frederick L. Jones points out that Maria Gisborne had nursed Mary Godwin after the death of her mother.

497 Jones, Howard Mumford. REVOLUTION AND ROMANTICISM. Harvard University Press, 1974.

Howard Mumford Jones states that, as the eighteenth century drew to a close, it produced many books and pamphlets advocating the emancipation of women. Mary Wollstonecraft's VINDICATION OF THE RIGHTS OF WOMAN is purely eighteenth century, if revolutionary, in its thinking. Sexual ecstacy plays no part in it and it has in common with romantic individualism only its emphasis on "freedom." Mary Wollstonecraft is no **romantic** and she resembles Voltaire's amie who knew about Newton and chemistry rather than the romantic woman of the feminine mystique.

498 Jong, Erica. "Dear Marys, Dear Mother, Dear Daughter," LOVEROOT. New York: Holt, Rinehart and Winston, 1975.

A section of the poem concerns Mary Wollstonecraft and Mary Shelley. Erica Jong refers to the circumstances of Wollstonecraft's death in childbirth.

499 Kamm, Josephine. RAPIERS AND BATTLEAXES: THE WOMEN'S MOVEMENT AND ITS AFTERMATH. London: Allen & Unwin Ltd., 1966.

The main events of Wollstonecraft's life are briefly described. A VINDICATION OF THE RIGHTS OF WOMAN is considered to be, like Wollstonecraft herself, flamboyant, passionate, and sentimental; yet it is a sincere and moving plea for a genuine partnership between men and women.

500 Keiser, Robert. "Die aufnahme englischen Schrifttums in der deutschen schweiz von 1830 bis 1860," ZURCHER BEITRAGE ZUR VERGLEICHENDEN LITERATURGESCHICHTE, X, 1962.

The article concerns the reception of English works in Switzerland between 1830 and 1860. It discusses the works of Wollstonecraft.

501 Kenton, Edna. "The Pap We Have Been Fed On: I. The First
     Free Woman in Fiction," BOOKMAN, XXXIX, June 1914, 467-71.

     This discussion of THE WRONGS OF WOMAN: OR MARIA stresses
     that it is more successful as propaganda than as novel.
     Despite its flaws, however, the novel is seen as important
     because it portrays a strong female character and empha-
     sizes a woman's right to sexual and economic equality.

502 Killham, John. TENNYSON AND THE PRINCESS: REFLECTIONS OF
     AN AGE. London: The Athlone Press, 1958.

     Wollstonecraft is mentioned briefly in Killham's discussion
     of feminist ideas. He stresses how little of Wollstonecraft
     was known by the age of Tennyson.

503 Kitano, Daikichi. "Burke Hakuron toshite no Jinken-ron:
     Wollstonecraft Kenkyu (The Rights of Men as a Refutation
     against Burke: A Study of Wollstonecraft)," SHOGAKU-HYORON,
     IX, II, 1930.

504 Kitano, Daikichi. FUJIN-UNDO NO KAISO MARY WOLLSTONECRAFT:
     KANOJO NO SHOGAI TO SHISO (MARY WOLLSTONECRAFT AS A PIONEER
     OF A FEMINIST MOVEMENT: HER LIFE AND IDEAS). Tokyo: Chik-
     ura-shobo, 1930.

     The book concerns Wollstonecraft as the founder of the
     movement of women's emancipation. Her life and works are
     described.

505 Kitano, Daikichi. "Mary Wollstonecraft no Joken-bengoron
     (A Vindication of the Rights of Woman by Mary Wollstone-
     craft)," SHOGAKU-HYORON, VIII, II, 1929.

506 Kramnick, Miriam Brody. Introduction to Wollstonecraft's
     VINDICATION OF THE RIGHTS OF WOMAN. Harmondsworth: Penguin,
     1975.

     Miriam Brody Kramnick outlines Wollstonecraft's life and
     relates it to the interests and illustrations of her VINDI-
     CATION OF THE RIGHTS OF WOMAN. She discusses fully the po-
     litical context of the polemical works and sets THE RIGHTS
     OF WOMAN against its feminist background. Finally, she
     traces Wollstonecraft's ideas through the nineteenth and
     twentieth centuries.

507 Kurtz, Benjamin P. and Carrie C. Autrey, ed. FOUR NEW LET-
     TERS OF MARY WOLLSTONECRAFT AND HELEN MARIA WILLIAMS. Berk-
     eley: University of California Press, 1937.

     The introduction traces the history of the four letters and
     describes how they were recovered. It provides short his-
     tories of the senders and receiver of the letters, as well
     as an enthusiastic character sketch of Mary Wollstonecraft.

A VINDICATION OF THE RIGHTS OF WOMAN is called one of the
sanest and best written of all the documents in the feminist movement.

508   Kurushima, Kyoko. "Feminism ni tsuite no Ichi-kosatsu:
       Wollstonecraft no Hito to Shiso (A Reflection on Feminism:
       Wollstonecraft and her Idea)," OKAYAMAKENRITSU TANKI-DAIG-
       AKU KENKYU KIYO, XIV, 1970.

509   Langdon-Davies, John. A SHORT HISTORY OF WOMEN. New York:
       Viking Press, 1927.

       John Langdon-Davies considers that the publication date of
       A VINDICATION OF THE RIGHTS OF WOMAN is as important in the
       history of women as the Renaissance and Reformation in the
       history of men. He gives the date of publication as 1774.

510   Laski, Marghanita. "Mary Quite Contrary," OBSERVER, Sep-
       tember 8, 1974, 27.

       In her review of Claire Tomalin's biography of Wollstone-
       craft, Marghanita Laski criticizes the way in which Woll-
       stonecraft has become an object of hagiolatry for some
       women. She praises Tomalin for her understanding that
       Wollstonecraft's views on the position of women resulted
       less from outrage at the injustice of women's status in
       general than from what she felt to be the unjust depriva-
       tions of her own situation. Laski states that Wollstone-
       craft's life ended when she had at last attained what all
       her life she had really wanted--marriage, security and re-
       spectability.

511   Lawrence, Margaret. THE SCHOOL OF FEMININITY: A BOOK FOR
       AND ABOUT WOMEN AS THEY ARE INTERPRETED THROUGH FEMININE
       WRITERS OF YESTERDAY AND TODAY. 1936; Port Washington,
       New York: Kennikat Press, 1966.

       A chapter on Wollstonecraft primarily gives a sketch of her
       life.

512   Leighton, Margaret. SHELLEY'S MARY: A LIFE OF MARY GODWIN
       SHELLEY. New York: Farrar, Straus and Giroux, 1973.

       This account of the life of Mary Shelley opens with a des-
       cription of the portrait of Mary Wollstonecraft which hung
       over the mantel in Godwin's house. Wollstonecraft is men-
       tioned several times in the book.

513   L'Esperance, Jean. TIMES LITERARY SUPPLEMENT, September 13,
       1974, 979.

       This is a letter concerning Richard Cobb's review of Claire
       Tomalin's LIFE AND DEATH OF MARY WOLLSTONECRAFT. It com-
       plains of the review's bias and inaccuracy and defends Woll-
       stonecraft.

514 LIBRARY OF CONGRESS. "List of References on Mary Wollstonecraft Godwin," 1922.

The list contains 46 items.

515 Lincoln, Anthony. SOME POLITICAL AND SOCIAL IDEAS OF ENG-
LISH DISSENT 1763-1800. Cambridge: at the University Press,
1938.

Anthony Lincoln discusses the judge in Wollstonecraft's
WRONGS OF WOMAN; OR MARIA, considering him a caricature of
Braxfield.

516 Linford, Madeline. MARY WOLLSTONECRAFT (1759-1797). London: Leonard Parsons (The Roadmaker Series), 1924.

In her biography, Madeline Linford places Wollstonecraft in
a feminist tradition. She states that, more than any other
person, Wollstonecraft pointed the way to the enfranchise-
ment of women and the recognition of their rights as human
beings. Although Wollstonecraft's work was ridiculed in
her life and scorned after her death, it later became a
foundation for the women's movement. Linford describes the
events of Wollstonecraft's life and comments on her works.

517 Littlewood, S. R. ELIZABETH INCHBALD AND HER CIRCLE: THE
LIFE OF A CHARMING WOMAN (1753-1821). London: Daniel
O'Connor, 1921.

S. R. Littlewood mentions Elizabeth Inchbald's resentment
over Godwin's marriage to Wollstonecraft.

518 Liversage, Toni. MARY OG REVOLUTIONEM. EN HISTORISK COL-
LAGE OM MARY WOLLSTONECRAFT, FORFATTEREN, TIL "ET FORSVAR
FOR KVINDERNES RETTIGHEDER." København: Gyldendal, 1974.

519 Loomis, Emerson Robert. "The Godwin's in THE LETTERS OF
SHAHCOOLEN," NINETEENTH-CENTURY FICTION, XVII, June 1962,
78-80.

Emerson Loomis' article concerns the American work entitled THE LETTERS OF SHAHCOOLEN, which was written to discredit radical British ideas and to expose their harmful
effects on America. The book aims primarily at Mary Wollstonecraft, who is seen as wanting to strip women of everything feminine. She is attacked for her ideas, which
are summarized in an extremely hostile and sarcastic way,
and for her personal character. The facts of her life
which the author uses seem to have derived from Godwin's
MEMOIRS.

520 Loomis, Emerson Robert. "The Turning Point in Pope's Repu-
     tation: A Dispute Which Preceded the Bowles-Byron Contro-
     versy," PHILOLOGICAL QUARTERLY, April 1963, 242-248.

     Emerson Loomis' article concerns the debate on the reputa-
     tion of Alexander Pope which broke out shortly after the
     publication of THE LYRICAL BALLADS. It discusses the sa-
     tirical poem of Thomas J. Mathias, who made his character,
     Pope, praise the current government and attack all those
     who dissented. In the course of the poem, Mary Wollstone-
     craft is criticized for forgetting the character and deli-
     cacy of her sex.

521 Lovett, Robert Morss and Helen Sard Hughes. THE HISTORY OF
     THE NOVEL IN ENGLAND. Boston: Houghton Mifflin Company,
     1932.

     In a section concerning fiction of the revolutionary era,
     there is mention of Wollstonecraft's MARY, A FICTION and
     THE WRONGS OF WOMAN. The novels are said to be interest-
     ing for their autobiographical significance.

522 Lucas, E. V. Preface to ORIGINAL STORIES by Mary Wollstone-
     crast. London: Henry Frowde, 1906.

     The preface briefly sketches Wollstonecraft's life and her
     pedagogical ideas.

523 Lundberg, Ferdinand and Marynia F. Farnham. MODERN WOMAN:
     THE LOST SEX. New York: Harper & Brothers, 1947.

     Ferdinand Lundberg and Marynia Farnham use Wollstonecraft
     as the epitome of the modern degenerate woman and the foun-
     der of feminism. They consider that the tenets of feminism
     may be traced to a single fateful book, A VINDICATION OF
     THE RIGHTS OF WOMAN. Psychoanalyzing Wollstonecraft, they
     find that she hates men and is afflicted with a severe case
     of penis envy. Lundberg and Farnham hold that Wollstone-
     craft's claim for equality with men means identity, and
     they endeavour to refute this claim by listing the distinc-
     tive sexual organs of the two sexes. They further try to
     discredit Wollstonecraft's theories by summarizing the
     facts of her life, which they have obtained from George
     Preedy's THIS SHINING WOMAN. In their view, the life reads
     like a psychiatric case history.

524 Luria, Gina. Introduction to Wollstonecraft works in THE
     FEMINIST CONTROVERSY IN ENGLAND 1788-1810. New York: Gar-
     land Publishing Inc., 1974.

     The introductions summarize Wollstonecraft's life and quote
     some modern critical opinions of the works.

525 Lutz, Alma. EMMA WILLARD, DAUGHTER OF DEMOCRACY. Boston
and New York, 1929.

The book mentions Emma Willard's opinions of Wollstonecraft.

526 McAleer, Edward C. THE SENSITIVE PLANT. Chapel Hill: University of North Carolina Press, 1950.

This is a biography of Margaret, Lady Mountcashel, Wollstonecraft's charge during her stay in Ireland. Wollstonecraft is mentioned frequently. Her relationships with Margaret and with Lady Kingsborough are discussed. Her THOUGHTS ON THE EDUCATION OF DAUGHTERS and ORIGINAL STORIES are summarized.

527 McAleer, J. J. BEST SELLER, XXXII, November 1972, 351.

This is a review of Eleanor Flexner's biography of Wollstonecraft.

528 MacCarthy, B. G. THE LATER WOMEN NOVELISTS 1744-1818. Cork: Cork University Press, 1947.

Wollstonecraft is discussed in a section on the didactic novel. Her life is summarized, and the main themes of A VINDICATION OF THE RIGHTS OF WOMAN noted. The primary interest, however, is in Wollstonecraft's three attempts at fiction, THE CAVE OF FANCY, MARY, A FICTION, and THE WRONGS OF WOMAN; OR MARIA. The novels are criticized for their autobiographical and polemical character, although MacCarthy points out that it is the propagandist purpose which occasionally galvanizes the stories into life. MacCarthy concludes that, although the novels are crude and confused, there are within them glimpses of power.

529 McClary, Ben Harris. Introduction to THE LETTERS OF SHAH-COOLEN. Gainesville; Scholars' Facsimiles & Reprints, 1962.

The introduction treats the attack on the life and character of Mary Wollstonecraft.

530 Maccoby, S. ENGLISH RADICALISM 1786-1832 FROM PAINE TO COBBETT. London: Allen & Unwin Ltd., 1955.

Wollstonecraft's VINDICATION OF THE RIGHTS OF WOMAN is described as a protest against the denial to women of equal intellectual training and opportunity with men. It is considered an interesting anticipation of much of the woman's rights movement of a century later. Maccoby believes, however, that it never cut as deeply as Godwin at his best.

531 MacGregor, Margaret Eliot. AMELIA ALDERSON OPIE: WORLDLING
AND FRIEND. Smith College Studies in Modern Languages, XIV,
1-2.

Margaret MacGregor refers to Wollstonecraft and mentions
Amelia Alderson's favorable comment on her.

532 McNiece, Gerald. SHELLEY AND THE REVOLUTIONARY IDEA. Cambridge: Harvard University Press, 1969.

In a chapter concerned with Shelley's reading on the French
Revolution, Gerald McNiece discusses Wollstonecraft's HIS-
TORICAL AND MORAL VIEW OF THE ORIGIN AND PROGRESS OF THE
FRENCH REVOLUTION. He notes Wollstonecraft's views, primarily that the morality of France had been destroyed by
the manners formed under the old government and that gradual reform was best, although sometimes violent revolutions
were inevitable. McNiece considers that Wollstonecraft's
ideas influenced Shelley.

533 Manley, Seon and Susan Belcher. O, THOSE EXTRAORDINARY WO-
MEN! OR THE JOYS OF LITERARY LIB. Philadelphia: Chilton
Book Company, 1972.

There is a biographical sketch of Wollstonecraft.

535 Meakin, Annette M. HANNAH MORE: A BIOGRAPHICAL STUDY.
London: Smith, Elder & Co., 1911.

Annette Meakin considers that Hannah More read Wollstonecraft's VINDICATION OF THE RIGHTS OF WOMAN.

536 Metzdorf, Robert F. THE TINKER LIBRARY. New Haven: The
Yale University Library, 1959.

The bibliography lists a letter from Wollstonecraft to Archibald Rowan written in April 1795 at Le Havre. It is printed
in W. Clark Durant's edition of Godwin's MEMOIRS OF MARY
WOLLSTONECRAFT. A first edition of Wollstonecraft's VINDI-
CATION OF THE RIGHTS OF WOMAN is also listed.

537 Mews, Hazel. FRAIL VESSELS: WOMAN'S ROLE IN WOMEN'S NOVELS
FROM FANNY BURNEY TO GEORGE ELIOT. London: The Athlone
Press, 1969.

In a chapter concerning the climate of opinion in the late eighteenth century, Hazel Mews briefly discusses Wollstonecraft's pedagogical works and her criticisms of the handbooks of advice of Gregory and Fordyce. A VINDICATION OF THE RIGHTS OF WOMAN is seen as Wollstonecraft's plea for the treatment of women as human beings; the book is praised for its honesty and moral courage.

538 Meynell, Alice. "Mary Wollstonecraft's Letters," PROSE AND POETRY, Ed. Frederick Page. London: Jonathan Cape, 1947.

This essay combines biographical data with an appreciation of both the public (A VINDICATION OF THE RIGHTS OF WOMAN) and the private (LETTERS TO IMLAY) writings of Mary Wollstonecraft, emphasizing that both are characterized by qualities that recommend Wollstonecraft's work over Godwin's.

539 Mineka, Francis E. THE DISSIDENCE OF DISSENT: THE MONTHLY REPOSITORY, 1806-1838. Chapel Hill: University of North Carolina Press, 1944.

Wollstonecraft is described as a Unitarian intellectual and the founder of the modern feminist movement.

540 Mizuta, Tamae. JOSEI KAIHO SHISO NO AYUMI (THE HISTORY OF FEMINIST IDEAS). Tokyo: Iwanami-shoten, 1973.

541 Mizuta, Tamae. "Mary Wollstonecraft ni okeru Risei to Kanjo; Igirisu Josei kaiho-shiso no Seiritsu (Reason and Sentiment in Mary Wollstonecraft: the Establishment of English Feminist Ideas)," SHAKAI-KAGAKU RONSHU, 1966.

542 Mizuta, Tamae. "Mary Wollstonecraft no Shoki no Shiso (An Early Thought of Mary Wollstonecraft)," ICHIMURA-GAKUEN TANKI DAIGAKU KAIGAKU KINENRONSO, 1965.

543 Morito, Tatsuo. "Godwin to Wollstonecraft tono Kekkon (The marriage between Godwin and Wollstonecraft)," WARERA, VII, X, and XI, 1925, 25-42.

The article concerns the married life of Godwin and Wollstonecraft. It notes the change in Godwin's views on marriage as they are revealed in his works.

544 Murry, John Middleton. Foreword to MEMOIRS OF MARY WOLLSTONECRAFT by William Godwin. London: Constable and Co., 1928.

The brief forword describes the MEMOIRS as the most intimate narrative we possess of the life of a woman of genius, courage, and beauty. Murry finds it ironical that the MEMOIRS which commemorated the woman whom Godwin loved should have been proof to his contemporaries of his moral turpitude.

545 Nason, Arthur H. Entry on Wollstonecraft in ENCYCLOPEDIA AMERICANA. New York, 1943.

This is a brief biographical sketch of Wollstonecraft. It is followed by a list of five works.

546 NATION, October 13, 1951, 313.

The review of Ralph Wardle's biography of Wollstonecraft criticizes the book for its professorial English and its banal conjectures and comments. The book is said, however, to include all the available facts about Wollstonecraft.

547 NEW CHAMPLIN CYCLOPEDIA FOR YOUNG FOLKS, ed. Lincoln Mac-Veagh. London: Hutchinson & Co., 1925.

Comment on Wollstonecraft is included.

548 NEW REPUBLIC, LXXII, October 19, 1932, 269.

The review of H. R. James's biography of Wollstonecraft compares it unfavorably to the work by Madeline Linford.

549 Newton, A. Edward. THE GREATEST BOOK IN THE WORLD AND OTHER PAPERS. Boston: Little, Brown, and Company, 1925.

In the chapter entitled "Skinner Street News," Wollstonecraft is characterized as a woman to be pitied, and her marriage to Godwin is described as the last in the series of misfortunes that made up her life. Newton is condescending toward Wollstonecraft's literary productions; A VINDICATION OF THE RIGHTS OF WOMAN is defined as harmless, reasonable, and rather coarse.

550 NEW YORK TIMES BOOK REVIEW, April 23, 1911, 245.

The review describes G. R. Stirling Taylor's biography of Wollstonecraft as a short and sympathetic account of its subject. Wollstonecraft's life is said to have been more than ordinarily lonely.

551 NEW YORK TIMES BOOK REVIEW, August 7, 1932, 9.

The review of H. R. James's biography of Wollstonecraft states that the biography succeeds in making its subject into a real person. The picture drawn is considered a dependable one, as Wollstonecraft appears in it in much the way she must have appeared to her intimates.

552 NEW YORKER, November 3, 1951, 155.

Ralph Wardle's biography is described as solid and workmanlike, although it is said to be overweight in its long discussion of Wollstonecraft's affair with Imlay.

553 Nicholes, Eleanor L. Introduction to A VINDICATION OF THE
RIGHTS OF MEN by Mary Wollstonecraft. Gainesville: Scholars' Facsimiles & Reprints, 1959.

Eleanor Louise Nicholes discusses the conceptual relationship between A VINDICATION OF THE RIGHTS OF MEN and A VIN-
DICATION OF THE RIGHTS OF WOMAN. She stresses Wollstonecraft's intellectual relationship with the Dissenters, especially with Richard Price, her first mentor. Nicholes
discusses briefly the difference between Wollstonecraft's
first and second editions of THE RIGHTS OF MEN. She notes
that Wollstonecraft expands a section criticizing ladies
of fashion. The subject would be treated further in THE
RIGHTS OF WOMAN. In her résumé of Wollstonecraft's life,
Nicholes makes several points of interest For example, she
notes that Eliza Wollstonecraft seems to have been pressured
into marriage by her brother Edward, who obtained the neces-
sary affidavit of consent from his father.

554 Nicholes, Eleanor L. "Mary Wollstonecraft," ROMANTIC REB-
ELS, ESSAYS ON SHELLEY AND HIS CIRCLE. Ed. Kenneth Neill
Cameron. Cambridge: Harvard University Press, 1973.

In her essay, Eleanor Nicholes sketches the events of Wollstonecraft's life. She follows the sketch with a consideration of the ideas and literary works. The personal nature
of Wollstonecraft's writing is stressed.

555 Nitchie, Elizabeth. "An Early Suitor of Mary Wollstonecraft," PMLA, LVIII, March 1943, 163-169.

Elizabeth Nitchie quotes a passage from THE MORNING HERALD
of London (July 23, 1827), describing the death of Joshua
Waterhouse. In it, there is the assertion that Waterhouse
paid his addresses to the once famous Mary Wollstonecraft
and that there exist letters to prove it. These have never
been found. Nitchie tries to place Waterhouse in Wollstonecraft's life, and she conjectures that the meeting between the two may have occurred in Bath or Bristol in the
summer of 1789 when Wollstonecraft was governess to the
daughters of Lord and Lady Kingsborough. Wollstonecraft's
letters of 1786 and 1787 reveal an emotional disturbance
of the sort a relationship with Waterhouse might have
caused. If the date of the meeting can be placed earlier,
it is possible that the effect of it is to be seen in Wollstonecraft's pedagogical work, THOUGHTS ON THE EDUCATION OF
DAUGHTERS, where she speaks of the misery of loving a person of whom one does not approve.

556 Nitchie, Elizabeth. MARY SHELLEY, AUTHOR OF "FRANKENSTEIN."
New Brunswick: Rutgers University Press, 1953.

Wollstonecraft is mentioned several times. Her pedagogical

ideas are briefly discussed. Elizabeth Nitchie stresses
Mary Shelley's devotion to Wollstonecraft's memory and discusses her fictional accounts of the motherless child.

557 Nixon, Edna. MARY WOLLSTONECRAFT: HER LIFE AND TIMES.
London: J. M. Dent and Sons, 1971.

Edna Nixon has written a popular biography whose factual
basis seems to be the biography of Ralph Wardle and the
1967 edition of the letters of Wollstonecraft and Godwin.
There is little evidence of original research. The context of Wollstonecraft's life is sketched.

558 Norman, Sylva. Introduction to LETTERS WRITTEN DURING A
SHORT RESIDENCE IN SWEDEN, NORWAY, AND DENMARK by Mary
Wollstonecraft. Fontwell, Sussex: Centaur Press, 1970.

In her brief introduction, Sylva Norman considers that the
LETTERS WRITTEN . . . IN SWEDEN are the most objective and
mature of Wollstonecraft's works. The lives of Wollstonecraft and Fanny Imlay, who accompanied her mother on her
travels, are outlined.

559 O'Malley, Ida Beatrice. WOMEN IN SUBJECTION: A STUDY OF
THE LIVES OF ENGLISHWOMEN BEFORE 1832. London: Duckworth,
1933.

An entire chapter devoted to Wollstonecraft defines her as
the earliest confessor of the women's movement. A VINDICA-
TION OF THE RIGHTS OF WOMAN is described as an apostolic
work that, had it been less hastily done, would have taken
its proper place among the world's great books. There is
praise for the literary qualities of Wollstonecraft's letters,
which link her to the Romantic tradition that followed her.

560 Orr, Lyndon. FAMOUS AFFINITIES OF HISTORY. New York: The
McClure Book Co. by Narper and Bros., 1912.

In an allusion to the "strange household" of William Godwin and Mary Wollstonecraft, Orr characterizes Mary Shelley
as inheriting both her mother's temperament and her powers
of mind.

561 Owen, Joan. LIBRARY JOURNAL, September 15, 1974, 2148.

Claire Tomalin's biography is described as strong and sob-
ering. It is said to be feminine without being feminist.
According to Joan Owen, it courageously and realistically
explores Wollstonecraft's various, often pathetic relationships and sets them within the context of her political
radicalism.

562 Pankhurst, Richard K. P. WILLIAM THOMPSON (1775-1833).
London: Watts & Co., 1911.

Richard Pankhurst finds Thompson's APPEAL TO ONE HALF OF
THE HUMAN RACE **more** practical and comprehensive than Wollstonecraft's VINDICATION OF THE RIGHTS OF WOMAN. He refers
to Thompson's admiration for Wollstonecraft and his criticism of the narrowness of her views.

563 Parker, D. L. CHRISTIAN SCIENCE MONITOR, September 1972,
13.

The review of Eleanor Flexner's biography of Wollstonecraft
finds the work disappointing. D. L. Parker dislikes Flexner's simplistic psychologizing and considers that Wollstonecraft is a far more complex personality than popular analysis
could make her.

564 Patterson, Sylvia W. ROUSSEAU'S EMILE AND EARLY CHILDREN'S
LITERATURE. Metuchen: New Jersey: The Scarecrow Press,
Inc., 1971.

A chapter concerns Wollstonecraft's book for children, ORIGI-
NAL STORIES.

565 Peabody, Josephine Preston. PORTRAIT OF MRS. W. A PLAY IN
THREE ACTS WITH AN EPILOGUE. Boston and New York: H. Houghton Mifflin Co., 1922.

According to Josephine Peabody, the aim of the play is to
bring into close range a name and a face. The foreword
sketches the events of Wollstonecraft's life. The play's
three acts deal with Wollstonecraft; the first is set in
John Opie's painting room in London in 1796 and the second
and third take place in the Polygon in 1797. The epilogue
concerns Godwin and his daughter, Mary, and is set in the
Polygon in 1814.

566 Pengelly, R. S. NOTES AND QUERIES, Series 12, X, January
7, 1922, 10-11.

In a reply to Durant's query (see 414) R. S. Pengelly
supplies two versions of an elopement intrigue involving Mary
Kingsborough and her cousin, Colonel Fitzgerald.

567 Pénigault-Duhet, P. M. "Du Nouveau sur Mary Wollstonecraft:
L'Oeuvre Littéraire de George Imlay," ETUDES ANGLAISES,
XXIV, 298-303.

P. M. Pénigault-Duhet questions why Godwin in his MEMOIRS
should not have mentioned Wollstonecraft's authorship of
THE EMIGRANTS and A TOPOGRAPHICAL DESCRIPTION OF THE WES-
TERN TERRITORY OF NORTH AMERICA. Although these books
were supposedly written by Gilbert Imlay, they have been

attributed to Wollstonecraft by some scholars (see 473).
Although Pénigault-Duhet notes the resemblance between THE
EMIGRANTS and Wollstonecraft's novel THE WRONGS OF WOMAN,
and between some of the incidents in THE EMIGRANTS and e-
vents in Wollstonecraft's life, she considers that it does
not prove Wollstonecraft's authorship. She points out
that the fictional incidents in THE EMIGRANTS resemble incidents in the life of Wollstonecraft's friend in Paris,
Helen Maria Williams. She considers Williams a more likely
candidate for the authorship.

568 Peter, Mary. "A Portrait of Mary Wollstonecraft Godwin by
     John Opie in the Tate Gallery," KEATS-SHELLEY MEMORIAL BUL-
     LETIN, XIV, 1963, 1-3.

     Mary Peter discusses Mary Wollstonecraft and the famous
     Opie portrait.

569 Pettingell, Phoebe. "The First Feminist," NEW LEADER,
     March 19, 1973, 19-20.

     In a review of Eleanor Flexner's biography, Phoebe Petting-
     gell states that Wollstonecraft's life has stood as an ex-
     ample to generations of feminists. She was, however, hardly
     a radical feminist by modern standards. Her life is said to
     have more than historical significance, for her struggle is
     the struggle of every intelligent woman.

570 Phillips, M. and W. S. Tomkinson. ENGLISH WOMEN IN LIFE
     AND LETTERS. 1926; New York: Benjamin Blom, Inc., 1971.

     Wollstonecraft is mentioned as a governess and founder of
     a private school.

571 Plumb, J. H. NEW STATESMAN, September 6, 1974, 320.

     In his review of Tomalin's biography of Wollstonecraft,
     J. H. Plumb states that there is no better book for an in-
     terpretation of Wollstonecraft. The biography is described
     as wise, penetrating and sympathetic. It is praised for
     its illumination of the radical world of the 1780s and
     1790s.

572 Pollin, Burton R. EDUCATION AND ENLIGHTENMENT IN THE WORKS
     OF WILLIAM GODWIN. New York: Las Americas Publishing Com-
     pany, 1962.

     Burton Pollin notes the effect on Godwin of Mary Wollstone-
     craft's ideas. Several of these are summarized in the
     course of the book.

573 Pollin, Burton R. "A Federalist Farrago," SATIRE NEWS-
     LETTER, IV, Fall 1966, 29-34.

     The article includes discussion of Federalist satire on
     Godwin and Mary Wollstonecraft.

574 Pollin, Burton R. GODWIN CRITICISM. A SYNOPTIC BIBLIOG-
RAPHY. Toronto: University of Toronto Press, 1967.

Many entries concern Wollstonecraft as well as Godwin.

575 Pollin, Burton R. "Mary Hays on Women's Rights in the
MONTHLY MAGAZINE," ETUDES ANGLAISES, XXIV, 271-282.

Burton Pollin discusses Mary Hays's reviews in the MONTHLY
MAGAZINE, especially her review of Mary Wollstonecraft's
LETTERS WRITTEN . . . IN SWEDEN. In this review, Hays
criticizes two phrases which she feels vitiate the effec-
tiveness of the work of the eminent author. Hays later
wrote Wollstonecraft's obituary for the MONTHLY MAGAZINE,
but omitted Wollstonecraft from her FEMALE BIOGRAPHY of
1803. According to Pollin, this is a reasonable omission,
since the biographies included are those of the illustrious
dead of the distant past.

576 Pollin, Burton R. "The Significance of Names in the Fiction of William Godwin," REVUE DES LANGUES VIVANTES,
XXXVII, IV, 1971, 388-399.

The article mentions Godwin's use of Wollstonecraft's name
in his novels.

577 Poston, Carol H. "Mary Wollstonecraft's A VINDICATION OF
THE RIGHTS OF WOMAN: A Critical and Annotated Edition."
Dissertation. Nebraska, 1973.

Carol Poston claims to have recorded the variants between
the first and second editions of A VINDICATION OF THE RIGHTS
OF WOMAN and to have identified the quotations and allusions
in the text. The introduction presents the historical and
intellectual milieu of THE RIGHTS OF WOMAN, a discussion of
the work as an educational tract, and an evaluation of Wollstonecraft's influence on others.

578 Potter, Simeon. TIMES LITERARY SUPPLEMENT, September 13,
1974, 979.

A letter concerning Richard Cobb's review of Claire Tomalin's
LIFE AND DEATH OF MARY WOLLSTONECRAFT defends the antiquity
of Wollstonecraft's surname.

579 Preedy, George R., pseud. Mrs. Gabrielle Long. THIS SHINING
WOMAN: MARY WOLLSTONECRAFT GODWIN. London: Collins, 1937.

George R. Preedy has written a fictionalized biography of
Wollstonecraft. It is probably the most hostile of the
many biographies, although it does not live up to the hostility of its foreword, where Preedy states that Wollstonecraft is famous only because she is a woman and that her
ideas are platitudinous and dull.

580 Previté-Orton. "Political Writers and Speakers," THE CAM-
BRIDGE HISTORY OF ENGLISH LITERATURE. Ed. Sir A. W. Ward
and A. R. Waller. Cambridge: at the University Press, 1914.

The author sketches Mary Wollstonecraft's life. He describes her liaison with Gilbert Imlay as the mistake of her
life. A VINDICATION OF THE RIGHTS OF WOMAN is said to be
primarily a plea for educational reform; it urged schemes
which were practicable if not necessarily advisable. The
opposition to the book was due not only to its definite
proposals, but also to its attacks on women and to the
coarseness of the descriptions of social evils. It is
judged important not as a literary work but as a landmark
in the evolution of social ideas.

581 Price, Mary Bell, and Lawrence M. THE PUBLICATION OF ENG-
LISH HUMANIORA IN GERMANY IN THE EIGHTEENTH CENTURY. Uni-
versity of California Publications in Modern Philology,
XLIV, 1955.

The book lists translations into German of Wollstonecraft's
works.

582 Pritchett, V. S. "The Strength of an Injured Spirit," THE
NEW YORK REVIEW, November 1972, 8-11.

In his review of Eleanor Flexner's biography of Wollstonecraft, V. S. Pritchett summarizes some of the biographical
information given by Flexner. He stresses the importance
of women novelists in the creation of a climate for Wollstonecraftian feminism.

583 Proper, C. B. A. SOCIAL ELEMENTS IN ENGLISH PROSE FICTION.
Amsterdam: H. J. Paris, 1929.

Proper suggests that Wollstonecraft be remembered less for
her fiction than for her polemical works and her letters.
A VINDICATION OF THE RIGHTS OF WOMAN is said to draw its
strength from the extreme forms of emotional stress under
which it was written.

584 PUBLISHERS WEEKLY, July 23, 1973, 71.

This is a note on the Penguin edition of Eleanor Flexner's
biography of Wollstonecraft.

585 Raine, Kathleen. WILLIAM BLAKE. New York: Praeger Publishers, 1971.

Kathleen Raine considers that, on the slender internal evidence of "Mary" and VISIONS OF THE DAUGHTERS OF ALBION, it
is possible to see an attraction by Blake toward Wollstonecraft, whose views on free love he shared. Raine points
out similarities between the thinking of Wollstonecraft and
Blake.

586 READER'S DICTIONARY OF AUTHORS. Ed. Harry Morgan Ayres.
New York: Knickerbocker Press, 1917.

There is a biographical note on Wollstonecraft.

587 Reich, Emil. WOMAN THROUGH THE AGES. London: Methuen, 1908.

Emil Reich describes A VINDICATION OF THE RIGHTS OF WOMAN as
a crude, assertive, and original book.

588 Renwick, W. L. ENGLISH LITERATURE 1789-1815. Oxford: at
the Clarendon Press, 1963.

In a discussion of Maria Edgeworth's LEONORA, Wollstonecraft
is briefly mentioned.

589 Riegel, Robert E. AMERICAN FEMINISTS. Lawrence: University
of Kansas Press, 1963.

Although acknowledged as a sourcebook for later feminists,
A VINDICATION OF THE RIGHTS OF WOMAN is said to have scandal-
ized the American public by its forthright treatment of female sexuality, and, according to Riegel, Wollstonecraft's
own life perpetuated the scandal.

590 Robertson, John M. PIONEER HUMANISTS. London: Watts, 1907.

Mary Wollstonecraft is one of the eight humanists discussed.
John Robertson pleads for a woman to write a worthy book on
Mary Wollstonecraft. He mentions her literary works, describing their greatness and their stylistic and organiza-
tional faults. Robertson finds Wollstonecraft least successful in her novels and in her book on the French Revolution. Some charges against Wollstonecraft are summarized
and Robertson provides a defense, especially to the charge
of immorality.

591 Robinson, Victor. WILLIAM GODWIN AND MARY WOLLSTONECRAFT.
New York: The Altrurians, 1907.

Victor Robinson presents Wollstonecraft as a perfect woman,
good, great, generous, and unafraid. Her VINDICATION OF
THE RIGHTS OF WOMAN is considered to be a book which shook
the world. Robinson sees Wollstonecraft working to rid
people of the idea of the unclean nature of sex. He praises
her for her understanding that women's freedom requires
their economic freedom. He ends with a rhetorical plea for
an appreciation of Wollstonecraft. There are several factual errors in his brief account of her life.

592 Roddier, Henri. J.-J. ROUSSEAU EN ANGLETERRE AU XVIII[E]
SIECLE: L'OEUVRE ET L'HOMME. Paris: Boivin & Cie, 1950.

Henri Roddier refers to Wollstonecraft's indignation against
Rousseau's ideas of female behavior, and also to her admiration of his egalitarian ideas.

593 Rodgers, Betsy. GEORGIAN CHRONICLE: MRS. BARBAULD AND HER
     FAMILY. London: Methuen & Co., Ltd., 1958.

     Wollstonecraft is mentioned briefly in two of the Barbaulds'
     letters.   One states that, if she had a magazine written
     entirely by women, Mrs. Barbauld would certainly exclude
     Mary Wollstonecraft from the staff.

594 Roper, Derek. "Mary Wollstonecraft's Reviews," NOTES AND
     QUERIES, V, 37-38.

     Roper questions the conclusions of Ralph Wardle concerning
     the authorship of the reviews in the ANALYTICAL REVIEW (see
     676). Roper considers that Wardle's assumption, that con-
     secutive reviews before a single initial were written by
     the same author, is unlikely. He bases his view on the
     large variety of topics treated in consecutive reviews.
     Roper concludes that the farther a review is from the fi-
     nal signature the less likely it is to be connected with
     that signature. Of the 412 reviews Wardle assigned to
     Wollstonecraft, Roper concludes that the 204 signed
     M or W are Wollstonecraft's, The other 208 have varying
     degrees of authenticity.

595 Ross, Margaret. "Mary and Margaret: The Triumph of Woman."
     Dissertation. Cornell, 1973.

     The dissertation is described as a "psychobiography" of
     Mary Wollstonecraft and Margaret Fuller. Wollstonecraft
     is seen as suffering emotional turmoil in her effort to
     exist in the world of men. In A VINDICATION OF THE RIGHTS
     OF WOMAN, Wollstonecraft relates her own personal conflicts
     to public issues. In the relationship with William Godwin,
     Wollstonecraft realizes her dream of living as an intellec-
     tual and emotional mate with a man.

596 Rossi, Alice S. THE FEMINIST PAPERS: FROM ADAMS TO DE BEAU-
     VOIR. New York: Columbia University Press, 1973.

     Excerpts from Wollstonecraft's VINDICATION OF THE RIGHTS OF
     WOMAN are included. An introduction summarizes the events
     of Wollstonecraft's life and relates THE RIGHTS OF WOMAN to
     its predecessor, Catherine Macaulay's LETTERS ON EDUCATION.

597 Roussin, Henri. WILLIAM GODWIN (1756-1836). Paris: Lib-
     rairie Plon, Plon-Nourrit et Cie., 1913.

     Henri Roussin describes the Wollstonecraft-Godwin marriage
     as a psychological enigma, for Wollstonecraft was all sen-
     timent and Godwin all reason. Roussin gives a brief sketch
     of Wollstonecraft's life, concentrating on her relationship
     with Godwin. He describes the hostile reaction to Godwin's
     MEMOIRS. The influence of Wollstonecraft on Godwin's ideas
     is noted.

598 Rover, Constance. LOVE, MORALS AND THE FEMINISTS. London: Routledge & Kegan Paul, 1970.

Constance Rover discusses the way in which the feminists were affected by their personal relationships, especially their disappointments in love. She suggests that Wollstonecraft's associations with Godwin and Imlay augmented the connection in the public mind between feminism and immorality.

599 Rusk, Ralph Leslie. "The Adventures of Gilbert Imlay,"UNIVERSITY OF INDIANA STUDIES, X, March 1923.

The life of Gilbert Imlay is sketched.

600 Sage,Lorna. "Rights and Wrongs: On Mary Wollstonecraft," ENCOUNTER, December 1974, 67-72.

In a review of Claire Tomalin's biography of Wollstonecraft, Lorna Sage describes the life as a mess and a muddle. Wollstonecraft is said to have continued to compromise most of her reasoned arguments about the rights of woman and to have shown in her life an almost indecent lack of poise. Sage considers, however, that the muddle of the life was neces-sary: Wollstonecraft believed that social change had to be made, and that the making involved wrecking. The damage she did to herself and others is not justified, but it can be seen as part of the whole process of change.

601 Saintsbury, George. THE PEACE OF THE AUGUSTANS: A SURVEY OF EIGHTEENTH CENTURY LITERATURE AS A PLACE OF REST AND RE-FRESHMENT. London: Oxford University Press, 1946.

Wollstonecraft is briefly mentioned in a section on revolutionary writers.

602 Sanders, Marion K. "A Slight Case of Library Fever or, How Not to Write a Book," HARPER'S MAGAZINE, 224, April 1962, 68-71.

The article concerns Marion Sanders' research in the New York Public Library for a popular biography of Mary Wollstonecraft.

603 SAN FRANCISCO CHRONICLE. October 21, 1951, 14.

Ralph Wardle's presentation of Wollstonecraft in his biography is described as a brilliant portrayal of her personality.

604 Sapiro, Virginia. "Feminist Studies and the Discipline: A Study of Mary Wollstonecraft," UNIVERSITY OF MICHIGAN PAPERS IN WOMEN'S STUDIES, Vol. I, No. I, February, 1974, 178-200.

Virginia Sapiro uses Wollstonecraft as an example of her contention that we must integrate thought on women into an intellectual and political background. She briefly relates the events of Wollstonecraft's life and summarizes A VINDICATION OF THE RIGHTS OF WOMAN, concentrating on the feminist and educational arguments. Sapiro then looks at the book as a product of the utilitarian and radical philosophy of the late eighteenth century. She asserts that, if Wollstonecraft is not viewed as part of an intellectual movement, much of THE RIGHTS OF WOMAN will seem unintelligible.

605 SATURDAY REVIEW, CII, September 1906, 294.

This is a review of a 1906 edition of Wollstonecraft's ORIGINAL STORIES. Wollstonecraft is described as an unattractive personality, although the reviewer points out that it was the difficulty of her life that made her so. ORIGINAL STORIES is considered ridiculously old-fashioned; if written during the reviewer's time, it would suggest insanity in the writer.

606 SATURDAY REVIEW, CXLIII, June 1927, 912.

This is a review of Godwin's MEMOIRS, edited by W. Clark Durant. It praises Durant's supplementary material and considers that the reissuing of the MEMOIRS will help to establish Wollstonecraft's reputation. Durant is described as a somewhat gushing and exuberant editor.

607 SATURDAY REVIEW, II, February 8, 1975, 29.

The review of Claire Tomalin's biography of Wollstonecraft summarizes the life. It describes the book as soundly researched and gracefully executed. It is mildly criticized for failing to question the integrity of Wollstonecraft's ideas but it is praised for its judicious appraisal of Wollstonecraft and its re-creation of her age.

608 Schlesinger-Eckstein. WILLIAM GODWIN, ERINNERUNGEN AN MARY WOLLSTONECRAFT. Halle; 1912.

This is a life of Wollstonecraft. It is appreciative, but not very scholarly. (See Pollin 3967).

609 Schneir, Miriam. FEMINISM: THE ESSENTIAL HISTORICAL WRITINGS. New York: Vintage Books, 1972.

An excerpt from A VINDICATION OF THE RIGHTS OF WOMAN is included. It is preceded by a short biographical introduction.

610 Schorer, Mark. WILLIAM BLAKE; THE POLITICS OF VISION. New York: Henry Holt & Co., 1946.

Mark Schorer considers the importance of Wollstonecraft's VINDICATION OF THE RIGHTS OF WOMAN for Blake's ideas on love and marriage. He describes Wollstonecraft as a kind of realist in a vividly sentimental age; she assumed the impermanence of passionate love, but insisted that marriage could be the foundation of social virtue.

611 Scott, Anne Firor. SOUTH ATLANTIC QUARTERLY, Fall 1973, 608.

In a short review of Eleanor Flexner's biography of Wollstonecraft, Anne Firor Scott says that Wollstonecraft's life, book, and influence have intrigued feminists since 1792. She quotes from Ruth Benedict's impressions of Wollstonecraft (see 342).

612 Séjourné, Philippe. ASPECTS GENEREAUX DU ROMAN FEMININ EN ANGLETERRE DE 1740 A 1800. Gap: Louis-Jean, 1966.

Philippe Séjourné sets Wollstonecraft the novelist among the other female novelists of her day. He finds her in many ways typical in her presentation of moral and material suffering. This is especially so in MARY, which Séjourné finds chiefly interesting for its references to Wollstonecraft's life. He finds THE WRONGS OF WOMAN more original. He praises its realism and frankness, in advance of the other novels of its time, and he singles out for special praise the narrative of Jemima, the lower class woman. Later in his book, Séjourné discusses the influence of A VINDICATION OF THE RIGHTS OF WOMAN on women novelists of the 1790s. He finds it especially strong in Mary Hays but present also in Mary Robinson.

613 Seligmann, Jean A. "The Toy Turns," NEWSWEEK, October 23, 1972, 105-106.

In a review of Eleanor Flexner's biography of Wollstonecraft, Jean Seligmann states that the biography is interesting less for what it tells us about Wollstonecraft the feminist than for what we learn about Wollstonecraft the woman.

614 Selincourt, Basil de. WILLIAM BLAKE. 1909; New York: Haskell House Publishers Ltd., 1971.

There is mention of Blake's illustrations of Wollstonecraft's ORIGINAL STORIES.

615 Serebrakova, Galina. NINE WOMEN, DRAWN FROM THE EPOCH OF THE FRENCH REVOLUTION. Trans. H. C. Stevens. London: Jonathan Cape, 1932.

The work includes a biographical sketch of Wollstonecraft.
The sketch contains many factual errors.

616 Shelley, Mary. THE LETTERS OF MARY WOLLSTONECRAFT SHELLEY.
Ed. Frederick L. Jones. Norman: University of Oklahoma
Press, 1944.

Mary Shelley makes several references to her mother and her
literary works in the course of her correspondence. In a
letter of June 1835, she states that Wollstonecraft had energy of character, but insufficient fire of imagination.
In a letter of May 1836, Mary Shelley refers to Wollstonecraft's tomb, which was opened for the burial of Godwin.

617 Shelley, Mary. MARY SHELLEY'S JOURNAL. Ed. Frederick L.
Jones. Norman: University of Oklahoma Press, 1947.

Many entries refer to Mary Shelley's reading of Wollstonecraft's works. Shelley states that, unlike her parents,
she is not a reformer and is not interested in the rights
of women.

618 Shelley, Percy Bysshe. LETTERS OF PERCY BYSSHE SHELLEY.
Ed. Roger Ingpen. London: Sir Isaac Pitman & Sons, Ltd.,
1909.

Wollstonecraft is mentioned briefly several times in Shelley's letters.

619 Shelley, Philip Allison. A SELECT ASSEMBLY OF NOTABLE BOOKS
AND MANUSCRIPTS FROM THE ALLISON-SHELLEY COLLECTION OF ANG-
LICA AMERICANA GERMANICA: AN EXHIBIT. Pennsylvania State
University Libraries, 1972.

This work includes a note on Wollstonecraft's translation
of Salzmann's ELEMENTS OF MORALITY.

620 Sheppard, R. Z. "Ms. Prometheus," TIME, January 13, 1975,
71.

In a review of Claire Tomalin's biography of Wollstonecraft,
R. Z. Sheppard gives a lively summary of the life and suggests that Mary Shelley may have had her mother in mind when
she created her "Modern Prometheus."

621 Shine, Hill. CARLYLE'S EARLY READING TO 1834. Lexington,
Kentucky, 1953.

There is a short discussion of Godwin's MEMOIRS.

622 Shirai, Atsushi. "Josei Kaiho no Senkusha tachi: France-
kakumei to Mary Wollstonecraft (Pioneers of Feminist Movement: French Revolution and Mary Wollstonecraft)," SHISO-
NO-KAGAKU, 118, 1971.

623 Shirai, Atsushi. "Joseikaiho-shisoshi-jo ni okeru Mary Wollstonecraft (Mary Wollstonecraft in the History of Feminist Ideas)," "MITAGAKKAI-ZASSHI, Vol. 62, No. 7, 1969.

The article points out the significance of Wollstonecraft's ideas in the history of European feminism.

624 Shirai, Atsushi. "Mary Wollstonecraft no Denki ni tsuite (On Mary Wollstonecraft Biography)," MITAGAKKI-ZASSHI, Vol. 63, No. 5 1970.

The article discusses biographies of Wollstonecraft, including Godwin's MEMOIRS.

625 Shirai, Atsushi. "Mary Wollstonecraft," SEKAI NO JOSEI SHI. Tokyo: Hyoron-sha, 1975.

626 Shirai, Atsushi. WILLIAM GODWIN KENKYU (A STUDY OF WILLIAM GODWIN). Tokyo: Mirai-sha, 1964, revised and enlarged edition, 1972.

627 Shirai, Takako and Atsushi. Introduction to MARY WOLLSTONE-CRAFT NO OMOIDE (MEMOIRS OF THE AUTHOR OF A VINDICATION OF THE RIGHTS OF WOMAN.) Tokyo: Mirai-sha, 1970.

628 Shirai, Takako. "Mary Wollstonecraft no Boseikan (Mary Wollstonecraft's view on Motherhood)," FUJIN MONDAI KONWAKAI KAIHO, 15, 1971.

629 Showalter, Elaine. WOMEN'S LIBERATION AND LITERATURE. New York: Harcourt Brace Jovanovich, Inc., 1971.

In her anthology, Elaine Showalter includes an excerpt from A VINDICATION OF THE RIGHTS OF WOMAN. A short introduction states that Wollstonecraft serves as an extreme ironic example of the treatment posterity accords a feminist writer, for she is remembered primarily for her relationship to Godwin and Shelley. THE RIGHTS OF WOMAN is said to have anticipated virtually all the demands of the woman's movement but to have been read by very few women in the nineteenth century

630 Simon, Hélène. "Godwins Ethik," ZUKUNFT, 66, February 1909, 381-385.

There is a discussion of Wollstonecraft's marriage with Godwin and her previous life. Her unhappiness is considered a result of the old morality of the family.

631 Simon, Hélène. WILLIAM GODWIN UND MARY WOLLSTONECRAFT. EINE BIOGRAPHISCH-SOZIOLOGISCHE STUDIE. München, 1909.

Hélène Simon sketches Wollstonecraft's life and literary career and discusses A VINDICATION OF THE RIGHTS OF WOMAN.

The book is praised for its originality and earnestness but
criticized for its lack of organization. Wollstonecraft is
considered an important influence on socialist thinkers of
her own and later ages.

632 Sitwell, Edith. ENGLISH WOMEN. London: William Collins,
     1932.

The book has a short chapter on Wollstonecraft. She is described as a woman of high ideals who battled to gain greater
opportunities for women. A VINDICATION OF THE RIGHTS OF WO-
MAN is called a strange book, because of the contrast between
the noble reasoning and the uncontrolled style.

633 Smith, Elton Edward and Esther Greenwell Smith. WILLIAM
     GODWIN. New York: Twayne Publishers, Inc., 1965.

Elton E. Smith and Esther G. Smith describe the relationship
between Godwin and Wollstonecraft and briefly sketch some of
the events of Wollstonecraft's previous life. They rely on
C. Kegan Paul and so perpetuate a few of the myths about
Wollstonecraft. They see Godwin's influence in Wollstonecraft's deepening radicalism toward the end of her life,
and they cite THE WRONGS OF WOMAN as evidence.

634 Snowden, Ethel. THE FEMINIST MOVEMENT. London: Collins
     Clear-Type Press, 1913.

Wollstonecraft's VINDICATION OF THE RIGHTS OF WOMAN is described as one of the text-books of the women's suffrage
movement. Wollstonecraft is said to have derived her ideas
in part from the French Revolution.

635 Southey, Robert. NEW LETTERS OF SOUTHEY. Ed. Kenneth
     Curry. New York: Columbia University Press, 1965.

Wollstonecraft is mentioned in several letters. In one of
1797, Southey describes Godwin's anger over a sermon which
included a false assertion about Wollstonecraft's death.
In a letter of 1798, Southey quotes Wollstonecraft's remark
on the superiority in cultivation of inland over coastal
dwellers; he states that this remark was as wise and true
as all of Wollstonecraft's remarks. In a letter of 1805,
Southey mentions that, while he disliked Godwin, he always
liked Wollstonecraft.

636 Spacks, Patricia Meyer. "'Ev'ry Woman is at Heart a Rake,'"
     EIGHTEENTH CENTURY STUDIES, VIII, no. I, 27-46.

Patricia Meyer Spacks discusses the presentation of sexual
passion by women writers. In the course of her discussion,
she briefly treats Wollstonecraft's first novel, MARY, A
FICTION. Spacks sees Wollstonecraft revolting against the
convention of sentimental novels and romances, that love
must triumph over all.

637 Spark, Muriel. PUBLIC OPINION, May 4, 1951.

In a review of David Fleisher's WILLIAM GODWIN, Muriel Spark mentions the influence of Wollstonecraft on Godwin's theories.

638 Stauffer, Donald A. THE ART OF BIOGRAPHY IN EIGHTEENTH CENTURY ENGLAND. Princeton: Princeton University Press, 1941.

Donald Stauffer discusses Godwin's MEMOIRS. He considers that the book is written with a beautiful sense of proportion, a unique standard of values, and a combination of sympathy with absolute frankness.

639 Stendhal, pseud. Henri Beyle. CORRESPONDANCE 1800-1821. Ed. Henri Martineau and V. del Litto. Paris, 1962.

Stendhal mentions Mary Wollstonecraft in a letter concerning the difference between the reputations of men and women.

640 Stenton, Doris Mary. THE ENGLISH WOMAN IN HISTORY. London: Allen & Unwin, 1957.

The book treats briefly Wollstonecraft's life and her VINDICATION OF THE RIGHTS OF WOMAN. Stenton considers that Wollstonecraft's ideas revealed in THE RIGHTS OF WOMAN were especially original and would have been accepted if they had been more moderately expressed. She finds Wollstonecraft too forceful in expression and too vague in her conceptions. The summary of the life includes many inaccuracies.

641 Steeves, Harrison R. BEFORE JANE AUSTEN: THE SHAPING OF THE ENGLISH NOVEL IN THE EIGHTEENTH CENTURY. London: George Allen & Unwin Ltd., 1966.

There are many references to Wollstonecraft and her presentation of eighteenth-century society. A VINDICATION OF THE rights of woman is described as a plea for educational opportunities for women. MARY, A FICTION is seen as a story of idealized passion; it is considered naive and feeble in the extreme. THE WRONGS OF WOMAN is judged more mature and it is important as an example of the fiction of purpose. It is, however, described as plodding and prosy.

642 Stephens, Winifred. WOMEN OF THE FRENCH REVOLUTION. London: Chapman & Hall Ltd., 1922.

Wollstonecraft is mentioned with other contemporary advocates of feminism.

643 Stevenson, Lionel. THE ENGLISH NOVEL: A PANORAMA. Boston: Houghton Mifflin Company, 1960.

Lionel Stevenson makes brief comments on MARY, A FICTION. It is described as an idealized autobiography of Wollstonecraft. It is criticized for its indulgence in passionate sensibility.

644 Stiles, Ezra. THE LITERARY DIARY OF EZRA STILES. Vol. III.
     Ed. Franklin Bowditch Dexter. New York: Charles Scribner's
     Sons, 1901.

     Two diary entries mention that Stiles read A VINDICATION OF
     THE RIGHTS OF WOMAN and knew of Mary Wollstonecraft's life
     and work through common acquaintances.

645 Stillman, Clara Gruening. NEW YORK HERALD TRIBUNE BOOKS,
     September 12, 1937, 20.

     In a review of George R. Preedy's THIS SHINING WOMAN and
     Benjamin P. Kurtz and Carrie C. Autrey's edition of NEW LET-
     TERS OF MARY WOLLSTONECRAFT AND HELEN M. WILLIAMS, Clara
     Stillman comments on the extremely different attitudes of
     the authors toward their subject. Preedy is critical of
     Wollstonecraft, stressing the relationship with Imlay and
     accusing her of behaving as frantically as if she had never
     written A VINDICATION OF THE RIGHTS OF WOMAN. The editors
     of NEW LETTERS, however, have an unbounded admiration for
     Wollstonecraft and they endow her with humor, sparkle, and
     fascination. The reviewer considers that Wollstonecraft is
     not a literary figure but she is an important pioneer of
     the woman's movement.

646 Storr, Marthe Severn. "L'Amour et le Mariage chez Godwin,"
     REVUE ANGLO-AMERICAINE, October 12, 1932, 31-47.

     Wollstonecraft's influence on Godwin's views on marriage
     and domesticity is discussed, as well as her lack of influ-
     ence on his concept of woman. After his marriage with Woll-
     stonecraft, Godwin continued to believe in the intellectual
     superiority of men over women. Marthe Severn Storr des-
     cribes the friendship and marriage of Godwin and Wollstone-
     craft and the public reactions to the news of the marriage.

647 Storr, Marthe Severn. MARY WOLLSTONECRAFT ET LE MOUVEMENT
     FEMINISTE DANS LA LITTERATURE ANGLAISE. Paris: Les Presses
     Universitaires de Paris, 1931.

     Marthe Severn Storr sets Wollstonecraft within her English
     and European context. She devotes a chapter to a summary
     of the events of her life and another to her character.
     The second part of the book concerns Wollstonecraft's works.
     The themes of these are stated and discussed under various
     headings, such as religion, reason, marriage, and education.
     All of Wollstonecraft's works are treated, but there is a
     concentration on A VINDICATION OF THE RIGHTS OF WOMAN and
     THOUGHTS ON THE EDUCATION OF DAUGHTERS, which is seen as
     prefiguring the more famous work in many respects. Woll-
     stonecraft is related to other thinkers of her time, espec-
     ially Godwin and Rousseau.

648 Streeter, Harold Wade. THE EIGHTEENTH CENTURY ENGLISH NOVEL
IN FRENCH TRANSLATION: A BIBLIOGRAPHICAL STUDY. New York:
Publications of the Institute of French Studies, Inc., 1936.

Wollstonecraft's WRONGS OF WOMAN appears as JEMIMA, OR THE
WRONGS OF WOMEN. It is described as an outspoken novel of
propaganda, based on the life of Wollstonecraft's sister.

649 Sullivan, Ruth. Ms., November 1975.

In her review of Jean Detre's A MOST EXTRAORDINARY PAIR,
Ruth Sullivan praises the book, while admitting that it
drags in places. She considers that Detre convincingly cap-
tures the eighteenth-century style and personality of Wollstonecraft.

650 Sunstein, Emily W. A DIFFERENT FACE: THE LIFE OF MARY WOLL-
STONECRAFT. New York: Harper & Row, 1975.

Emily Sunstein's biography relates the events of Wollstonecraft's life and sets them in their eighteenth-century context. Much information is given about the customs and concerns of the time, and various incidents in the lives of
Wollstonecraft and her family are illuminated by records of
those similarly placed. The book includes quotations from
Wollstonecraft's letters and those of her sisters and
friends, as well as from her novels MARY, A FICTION and THE
WRONGS OF WOMAN. The author frequently uses these novels in
her description of Wollstonecraft's relationships. The
character of Wollstonecraft is discussed throughout the book
and Sunstein finds and describes recurring psychological
patterns. There is little original research to take the
book beyond previous biographies, but there are original
conjectures, notably the one concerning Wollstonecraft's
brother Henry. The literary works are discussed and summarized in passing. There are short notes on the chapters
and a list of major sources.

651 Sunstein, Emily W. "Mary Wollstonecraft," TIMES LITERARY
SUPPLEMENT, October 4, 1974, 1078.

This is a letter in response to Richard Cobb's review of
Claire Tomalin's LIFE AND DEATH OF MARY WOLLSTONECRAFT. It
points out several inaccuracies in Cobb's review.

652 Taylor, G. R. Stirling. MARY WOLLSTONECRAFT: A STUDY IN
ECONOMICS AND ROMANCE. London: Martin Secker, 1911.

G. R. Stirling Taylor provides an enthusiastic retelling of
the events of Wollstonecraft's life. He sees her as an out-
cast and a pioneer in women's rights. He stresses her importance for his own century when he states that this pioneer of
the eighteenth century is still clearing a way for the twentieth. Taylor's initial chapter describes the condition of

women in Wollstonecraft's time and summarizes the roles of
women during the previous century. It also briefly mentions
earlier women writers, from Lucy Hutchinson to Fanny Burney.
In other chapters, Taylor sketches Wollstonecraft's life.
His attitudes toward its various events are closer to Godwin's than to Kegan Paul's. For instance, he reverts to the
Godwinian analysis of Wollstonecraft's religion and takes
Godwin's statements about the Fuseli affair as one more
proof of the existence of the affair Kegan Paul had tried to
deny. Taylor provides sympathetic portraits of Wollstonecraft's friends, such as Joseph Johnson and Richard Price.
There is some discussion of the works. Taylor sees A VINDI-
CATION OF THE RIGHTS OF WOMAN not as an attack on men but as
an attack on women on behalf of all humanity.

653 Thompson, E. P. THE MAKING OF THE ENGLISH WORKING CLASS,
     1963; Penguin Books, 1968.

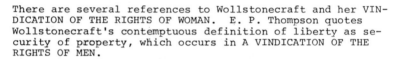

There are several references to Wollstonecraft and her VIN-
DICATION OF THE RIGHTS OF WOMAN. E. P. Thompson quotes
Wollstonecraft's contemptuous definition of liberty as se-
curity of property, which occurs in A VINDICATION OF THE
RIGHTS OF MEN.

654 Thornton, Richard H. NOTES AND QUERIES, Series 12, XII,
     April 28, 1923, 331.

This is a reprint of a letter, tentatively dated 1790, which
Wollstonecraft wrote to Joseph Johnson. In it she bemoans
her life as a governess and embraces her declining health as
a sign of imminent death and as a relief from her duties.

655 TIMES LITERARY SUPPLEMENT, April 15, 1926, 273.

This is a review of Ford K. Brown's WILLIAM GODWIN. The reviewer refers to the growing importance of Wollstonecraft
and hopes that her improving reputation will help Godwin's.

656 TIMES LITERARY SUPPLEMENT, June 23, 1927, 434.

This is a review of Durant's edition of Godwin's MEMOIRS.
The reviewer criticizes Durant for his tone in his intro-
ductory material and for the factual errors he makes. One
error concerns the dates of Wollstonecraft's stay in Paris.

657 TIMES LITERARY SUPPLEMENT, August 4, 1932, 552.

This review of H. R. James's biography of Wollstonecraft
considers the work too slight; it is said to miss the intense psychological interest of Wollstonecraft.

658 TIMES LITERARY SUPPLEMENT, February 20, 1937, 126.

The review of George Preedy's biography of Wollstonecraft
states that the author has drawn a sympathetic and convin-
cing portrait of her subject.

659 TIMES LITERARY SUPPLEMENT, September 11, 1953, 583.

In a review of R. G. Grylls's WILLIAM GODWIN, it is noted
that Grylls drops her ironic tone when dealing with Wollstonecraft.

660 TIMES LITERARY SUPPLEMENT, March, 1964, 224.

In "Notes on Sales," there is mention of two of Wollstonecraft's letters concerning her novel, THE WRONGS OF WOMAN.

661 TIMES LITERARY SUPPLEMENT, December 25, 1970, 1508.

This is a review of Margaret George's biography of Wollstonecraft and of the Centaur Press edition of LETTERS WRIT-
TEN . . . IN SWEDEN. The reviewer finds Wollstonecraft a
perfect example of the type of person who elevates every
deprivation to the status of dogma. LETTERS WRITTEN . . .
IN SWEDEN is described as a dullish volume.

662 Tobin, James E. EIGHTEENTH CENTURY ENGLISH LITERATURE AND
ITS CULTURAL BACKGROUND: A BIBLIOGRAPHY. New York: Fordham
University Press, 1939.

Twelve items are listed under Mary Wollstonecraft Godwin.

663 Tomalin, Claire. THE LIFE AND DEATH OF MARY WOLLSTONECRAFT.
London: Weidenfeld and Nicolson, 1974.

Claire Tomalin retells the story of Wollstonecraft's life
with some discussion of the literary works. She sets the
scenes of Wollstonecraft's early life and gives details a-
bout her family, especially about her sisters. Later peri-
ods of Wollstonecraft's life are also set in context, and
Tomalin pays special attention to the time with the Kings-
boroughs, who are discussed in detail, and to the time in
revolutionary France. Tomalin has a useful bibliography
and three appendices. The first concerns eighteenth-century
votes for women. The second is   a review of Mary Hays's
APPEAL TO THE MEN OF GREAT BRITAIN IN BEHALF OF WOMEN, which
Tomalin mistakenly believes to be lost. The third is a note
on Dickens, the Polygon and Harold Skimpole.

664 Tomory, Peter. LIFE AND ART OF HENRY FUSELI. London:
Thames and Hudson, 1972.

Peter Tomory's book on Fuseli repeats many of the old mistakes concerning Wollstonecraft. It states that Blake

wished Wollstonecraft to join his household and that she
wished to join Fuseli's. Wollstonecraft is considered the
inspiration of Fuseli's aphorism that the age of eunuchs is
the age of viragoes. Tomory also suggests that she was an
inspiration for Mad Kate. Several references in A VINDICA-
TION OF THE RIGHTS OF WOMAN are supposedly to Fuseli.

665   Tompkins, J. M. S. THE POLITE MARRIAGE. Cambridge: at the
University Press, 1938.

J. M. S. Tompkins briefly mentions Wollstonecraft as the
target of Richard Polwhele's satirical poem, where she appears as the deluder of other women. Tompkins also refers
to her friendship with Mary Hays, whom she influenced. Although always a feminist, Hays, according to Tompkins,
moved in later life from discipleship of Mary Wollstonecraft to harmony with Hannah More.

666   Tompkins, J. M. S. THE POPULAR NOVEL IN ENGLAND 1770-1800.
1932; Lincoln: University of Nebraska Press, 1961.

J. M. S. Tompkins briefly discusses Wollstonecraft's two
novels, MARY and THE WRONGS OF WOMAN; OR MARIA. The first
she sees as more like notes for a novel than a novel and,
although there is a promise of richness and depth in it,
this is never fulfilled. THE WRONGS OF WOMAN is discussed
among other philosophical novels of othe 1790s. Tompkins
finds it a crude but deeply interesting novel of propaganda.

667   Todd, Janet M. "The Polwhelean Tradition and Richard Cobb,"
STUDIES IN BURKE AND HIS TIME, XVI, III, Spring 1975, 271-
277.

The article concerns abusive criticism of Wollstonecraft,
from Richard Polwhele's THE UNSEX'D FEMALES to Richard Cobb's
review. It isolates certain characteristics of this criticism.

668   Todd, Janet M. Introduction to AN HISTORICAL AND MORAL VIEW
OF THE ORIGIN AND PROGRESS OF THE FRENCH REVOLUTION AND THE
EFFECT IT HAS PRODUCED IN EUROPE, By Mary Wollstonecraft.
New York: Scholars' Facsimiles & Reprints, 1975.

The introduction briefly sketches the events of Wollstonecraft's life before she arrived in Paris in 1792. It mentions reviews for the ANALYTICAL REVIEW that suggest some
of the ideas to be elaborated in THE FRENCH REVOLUTION. It
also alludes to previous Wollstonecraft works on France
that suggest the various attitudes toward France and its
Revolution she held between her arrival in Paris and her
writing of THE FRENCH REVOLUTION. The introduction summarizes the main ideas of the work and comments on its
sources and its style. It discusses Wollstonecraft's treatment of women in the book and contrasts this with the treatment in A VINDICATION OF THE RIGHTS OF WOMAN.

669 Todd, Janet M. "The Language of Sex in A VINDICATION OF THE
     RIGHTS OF WOMAN," MARY WOLLSTONECRAFT NEWSLETTER, I, II,
     April 1973, 10-17.

     The article discusses Wollstonecraft's use of the term "man."
     In the first chapter of THE RIGHTS OF WOMAN, "man" and "men"
     are synonymous with humanity, but in the second chapter,
     where male tyranny is considered, the terms come to exclude
     women. Occasionally in this chapter Wollstonecraft seems to
     search for a neutral term to replace "man" as humanity. The
     article also discusses Wollstonecraft's use of the terms
     "ladies," "gentlemen" and "masculine."

670 Tomkievicz, Shirley. "The First Feminist," HORIZON, XIV, 2,
     Spring 1972, 115-119.

     The article is primarily a biographical sketch of Wollstone-
     craft. She is described as the first person to speak at any
     length and to any effect about women's rights. She did not
     found the women's rights movement but she was its inspiration.

671 Utter, Robert Palfrey and Gwendolyn Bridges Needham. PAME-
     LA'S DAUGHTERS. New York: The MacMillan Company, 1936.

     A VINDICATION OF THE RIGHTS OF WOMAN is quoted for its de-
     nunciation of delicacy in women and later, in a chapter on
     the spinster figure in fiction, for its support of the eco-
     nomic independence of unmarried women achieved through edu-
     cation. Mary Wollstonecraft's influence is said to be im-
     portant for the evolution of feminism.

672 Voisine, Jacques-Rene. JEAN-JACQUES ROUSSEAU EN ANGLETERRE
     A L'EPOQUE ROMANTIQUE, LES ECRITS AUTOBIOGRAPHIQUES ET LA
     LEGENDE. Paris, 1956.

     There is some mention of Mary Wollstonecraft and her view
     of Rousseau. (See Pollin 4130).

673 Walling, William A. MARY SHELLEY. New York: Twayne Pub-
     lishers, Inc., 1972.

     Wollstonecraft is briefly discussed as the mother of Mary
     Shelley.

674 Wardle, Ralph M. HAZLITT. Lincoln: University of Nebraska
     Press, 1971.

     Ralph Wardle mentions Hazlitt's and Coleridge's impressions
     of Wollstonecraft.

675 Wardle, Ralph, ed. GODWIN AND MARY: LETTERS OF WILLIAM
     GODWIN AND MARY WOLLSTONECRAFT. Lawrence: University of
     Kansas Press, 1966.

     The introduction gives biographical details of the Godwin-

Wollstonecraft friendship and marriage. Ralph Wardle describes the letters he is printing as two people conversing
intimately.

676 Wardle, Ralph M. "Mary Wollstonecraft, Analytical Re-
     view," PMLA, LXII, December 1947, 100-109.

Wollstonecraft started contributing to the ANALYTICAL RE-
VIEW in 1788. According to Ralph Wardle, her sprawling
colloquial style contrasts with the periodic writing of
her colleagues. The reviews signed M and W are assigned
by Wardle to Wollstonecraft on the basis of style, of subject matter and of their disappearance in late 1792, when
Wollstonecraft went to France. Wardle considers that those
signed T are also probably by Wollstonecraft, since they
reveal Wollstonecraft's stylistic habits and disappear after
1792. In 1796, when Wollstonecraft settled again in London,
the M articles resume. There are 412 articles signed M, W,
and T. Wardle comments on the reviews, which he believes
add detail and perspective to our picture of a crucial period of Wollstonecraft's career.

677 Wardle, Ralph M. MARY WOLLSTONECRAFT: A CRITICAL BIOGRAPHY.
     1951; Lincoln: University of Nebraska Press, 1966.

Ralph Wardle relates the facts of Wollstonecraft's life,
quoting liberally from her letters. The facts come from
the Abinger collection of letters and materials concerning
Wollstonecraft, as well as from previous biographies and
accounts. The biography has copious notes, but no bibliography. Wardle provides information about Wollstonecraft's
contemporaries and about the society in which she lived.
He summarizes and discusses the literary works and places
them in their literary context. He expresses admiration
for Wollstonecraft's most famous books but he finds A VIN-
DICATION OF THE RIGHTS OF MEN dominated more by emotion than
by reason; it is a triumph of propaganda rather than critical analysis. A VINDICATION OF THE RIGHTS OF WOMAN is considered by Wardle to be a great book. He stresses its basis
in Wollstonecraft's experience, so that, although the arguments are not always original, the development and application of them are always so.

678 Wardle, Ralph M. "Mary Wollstonecraft Godwin," COLLIER'S
     ENCYCLOPEDIA. New York, 1962.

This is a short sketch of Wollstonecraft's life and an account of her death.

679 Warner, James A. "The Reaction in Eighteenth-Century Eng-
     land to Rousseau's two DISCOURS," PMLA, XLVIII, 1933, 471-
     487.

Wollstonecraft is briefly mentioned.

680 Wasser, Henry H. "Notes on the Visions of the Daughters Albion," MODERN LANGUAGE QUARTERLY, IX, 1948, 292-297.

Wasser traces some of Oothoon's questions on the subject of sexual freedom and restraint to Mary Wollstonecraft's VINDICATION OF THE RIGHTS OF WOMAN.

681 Watson, Pauline Sewell. "Mary Wollstonecraft: Author and Woman." MA Thesis. Iowa, 1935.

682 Waugh, Arthur. "Mary Wollstonecraft," BOOKMAN, LXXXII, 1932, 249.

The review of H. R. James's MARY WOLLSTONECRAFT: A SKETCH states that the work is not as full as other biographies; it has, however, a vivid quality and a sympathy that compensates for its thinness of detail. A short summary of Wollstonecraft's life is given.

683 Wedd, A. F. THE FATE OF THE FENWICKS: LETTERS TO MARY HAYS (1798-1828). London: Methuen & Co. Ltd., 1927.

A. F. Wedd speculates that Mary Hays and Eliza Fenwick may have been introduced to each other by Mary Wollstonecraft. Both were with her during her last days.

684 Wedd, A. F. THE LOVE-LETTERS OF MARY HAYS (1779-1780). London: Methuen & Co. Ltd., 1925.

In part I of this work, entitled "The Story of Mary Hays," A. F. Wedd traces Hays's relationship with Wollstonecraft. She describes the first meeting of the two women at Joseph Johnson's house and their later renewal of friendship after Wollstonecraft's return from France. A letter from Mr. Evans to Miss Hays, quoted by Wedd in the final section of her book, refers to Hays as a disciple of Wollstonecraft. The book includes several letters from Wollstonecraft to Hays.

685 Wellington, Amy. WOMEN HAVE TOLD: STUDIES IN THE FEMINIST TRADITION. Boston: Little, Brown, and Company, 1930.

There is a section on Wollstonecraft in a chapter entitled "Pioneers." Her life is described as turbulent and sorrowful and A VINDICATION OF THE RIGHTS OF WOMAN is considered an epoch-making book.

686 Welsberg, Elizabeth. LIBRARY JOURNAL, September 1970, 2793.

Margaret George's biography of Wollstonecraft is described as an in-depth study of a fascinating woman.

687 Whitmore, Clara H. WOMAN'S WORK IN ENGLISH FICTION FROM THE
     RESTORATION TO THE MID-VICTORIAN PERIOD. New York: G. P.
     Putnam's Sons, 1910.

     Mary Wollstonecraft is nowhere fully discussed in this book
     but she is mentioned frequently. Her life is judged to have
     been wrecked by the dream of a life of perfect freedom.
     There is a short biographical sketch.

688 Williams, Raymond. "Vindication of a radical," GUARDIAN
     WEEKLY, September 14, 1974, 22.

     In a review of Claire Tomalin's biography of Wollstonecraft,
     Raymond Williams states that Wollstonecraft was one of the
     very few radical thinkers to extend the concept of human
     rights to women. Williams notes in Wollstonecraft's repu-
     tation the "common syndrome," in which radical feminism and
     sexual license are seen as necessarily associated. Williams
     expresses admiration not only for the young puritan radical,
     which Wollstonecraft was when she wrote A VINDICATION OF THE
     RIGHTS OF WOMAN, but also for the developed, awakened, and
     still fighting woman and mother she later became.

689 Wilson, Arthur M. NEW YORK TIMES BOOK REVIEW, January 5,
     1975, 5.

     This is a review of Claire Tomalin's biography of Wollstone-
     craft. It summarizes the life and states that Wollstonecraft
     exemplified as well as argued for woman's rights. Wollstone-
     craft's tragedy is said to lie in the gap between her princi-
     ples and the emotions which developed after her liaison with
     Imlay. Claire Tomalin's biography is praised for bringing
     out the suffering inherent in this predicament.

690 Wilson, Jacobine Menzies and Helen Lloyd. AMELIA: THE TALE
     OF A PLAIN FRIEND. London: Oxford University Press, 1937.

     In this biography of Amelia Alderson, there is mention of the
     friendship between Alderson and Wollstonecraft. Alderson's
     admiration for Wollstonecraft is described.

691 Wilson, Mona. JANE AUSTEN AND SOME CONTEMPORARIES. London:
     Cresset Press, 1938.

     Mona Wilson compares Wollstonecraft and Jane Austen; she sees
     them both as rational women. Wollstonecraft and Austen
     praise the woman of sense and scorn the trivial elegant woman.

692 Wilson, Mona. THE LIFE OF WILLIAM BLAKE. New York: Oxford
     University Press, 1949.

     There is a brief account of Wollstonecraft's life. Mona Wil-
     son points out the similarity between Wollstonecraft's con-
     cerns in A VINDICATION OF THE RIGHTS OF WOMAN and those of
     Blake in VISIONS OF THE DAUGHTERS OF ALBION.

693 Wollstonecraft, Mary. GODWIN AND MARY: LETTERS OF WILLIAM
GODWIN AND MARY WOLLSTONECRAFT. Ed. Ralph Wardle. Lawrence:
University of Kansas Press, 1966.

Although Godwin published many of Wollstonecraft's letters
in POSTHUMOUS WORKS OF THE AUTHOR OF "A VINDICATION OF THE
RIGHTS OF WOMAN," he did not include 162 letters between
Wollstonecraft and himself. These were later divided into
3 lots, one of which came into Lord Abinger's collection.
It is these letters that Wardle prints in this volume. 76
letters are published for the first time and 30 have never
before been published in their entirety.

694 Wollstonecraft, Mary. FOUR NEW LETTERS OF MARY WOLLSTONE-
CRAFT AND HELEN MARIA WILLIAMS. Ed. Benjamin P. Kurtz and
Carrie C. Autrey. Berkeley: University of California Press,
1937.

In this book are printed three letters of Mary Wollstonecraft
to the American, Ruth Barlow. They were written from Havre
in 1794. The third letter announces the birth of Fanny and
describes Wollstonecraft's joy at being a mother. For the
introduction, see 507.

695 Woodress, James. A YANKEE'S ODYSSEY: THE LIFE OF JOEL BARLOW.
Philadelphia: Lippincott, 1958.

The book has some details of Mary Wollstonecraft's relationship with Joel Barlow.

696 Woody, Thomas. A HISTORY OF WOMEN'S EDUCATION IN THE UNITED
STATES. New York: The Science Press, 1929.

Mary Wollstonecraft is mentioned frequently for her important
role in the development of women's education. A VINDICATION
OF THE RIGHTS OF WOMAN is cited as a rebuttal to works on female education by Rousseau, Fordyce, De Stael, Gregory, and
others.

697 Woolf, Virginia. THE SECOND COMMON READER. 1932; Harcourt
Edition, 1965.

Virginia Woolf briefly sketches the events of Wollstonecraft's
life. She expresses her enthusiasm for Wollstonecraft and her
admiration of her marriage to Godwin. She concludes that
Wollstonecraft is, through the memory of her life, still an active influence on women.

698 Woolsey, Dorothy B. "Mary Wollstonecraft," NEW YORK HERALD
TRIBUNE BOOKS, September 26, 1937, 18.

This is a hostile review of George Preedy's biography of
Wollstonecraft, THIS SHINING WOMAN.

699 WORLD'S BEST LITERATURE. Ed. John W. Cunliffe and Ashley H. Thorndike. New York: Knickerbocker, 1917.

In a section entitled "Modern Ideal of Womanhood," there is an excerpt from Wollstonecraft's VINDICATION OF THE RIGHTS OF WOMAN. It is prefaced by a biographical sketch of Wollstonecraft. She is described as perhaps the most prophetic character of her time. She is considered to have been guided by her reason in her books but by her affections in her life.

700 Wright, Raymond, ed. PROSE OF THE ROMANTIC PERIOD 1780-1830. Harmondsworth: Penguin, 1956.

The book includes selections from Wollstonecraft.

701 Wright, Thomas. THE LIFE OF WILLIAM BLAKE. Olney: Thomas Wright, 1929.

Thomas Wright considers that, in a way, the heroine of VISIONS OF THE DAUGHTERS OF ALBION is Mary Wollstonecraft.

702 Wyatt, Edith. "The Progress of a Path-Finder," NORTH AMERICAN REVIEW, CCIV, August 1917, 292-303.

The short biographical section especially concentrates on Wollstonecraft's life with Imlay. Her tendency to idealize him is regarded as her one tragic flaw, and she is applauded for rebounding from her passionate quest of Imlay in order to construct a worthwhile life with Godwin, whose private role as step-father to Fanny is emphasized. A VINDICATION OF THE RIGHTS OF WOMAN is amply praised as the first book to advocate women's suffrage as well as co-education.

703 Wyzewa, Teodor. SOME WOMEN: LOVING OR LUCKLESS. Trans. C. H. Jeaffreson. London: John Lane, 1909.

A section on Wollstonecraft is entitled "The Mother of Feminism." Wollstonecraft is described as an apostle, the first to preach the war of the sexes and the revolt of woman against the yoke of man. A brief sketch of Wollstonecraft's life is given. Her marriage to Godwin is described as nothing more than a cordial friendship.

704 Yamakawa, Kikue. "Mary Wollstonecraft to sono Jidai (Mary Wollstonecraft and her Times)," GENDAI SEIKATSU TO FUJIN. Tokyo: Sobunkaku, 1919.

705 Zall, Paul M. "The Cool World of Samuel Taylor Coleridge: Joseph Johnson or the Perils of Publishing," WORDSWORTH CIRCLE, III, I, Winter 1972, 25-30.

The article mentions Mary Wollstonecraft as one of the writers Joseph Johnson aided.

ADDENDA

1788 - 1800

706 Neal, James Armstrong. AN ESSAY ON THE EDUCATION AND GENIUS
     OF THE FEMALE SEX. TO WHICH IS ADDED, AN ACCOUNT, OF THE COM-
     MENCEMENT OF THE YOUNG-LADIES' ACADEMY OF PHILADELPHIA, HELD
     THE 18TH OF DECEMBER, 1794; UNDER THE DIRECTION OF MR. JOHN
     POOR, A. M. PRINCIPAL. Philadelphia: Jacob Johnson & Co.,
     1795.

     Wollstonecraft is mentioned by a schoolgirl as one who had
     asserted and vindicated the rights of her sex.

1800 - 1900

707 Carter, Elizabeth. MEMOIRS, Ed. Rev. Montagu Pennington.
     London: Printed for F. C. and J. Rivington, 1807.

     Elizabeth Carter is said to have detested the principles
     and wild theories of Mary Wollstonecraft.

708 Drinker, Elizabeth. EXTRACTS FROM THE JOURNAL OF ELIZABETH
     DRINKER, FROM 1759 TO 1807. Ed. Henry D. Biddle. Philadel-
     phia: J. B. Lippincott, 1889.

     Elizabeth Drinker comments on A VINDICATION OF THE RIGHTS OF
     WOMAN. She considers herself near to Wollstonecraft in many
     opinions, although she states that she does not advocate
     quite so much independence.

709 ENCYCLOPAEDIA AMERICANA. A POPULAR DICTIONARY OF ARTS, SCI-
     ENCES, LITERATURE, HISTORY, POLITICS, AND BIOGRAPHY . . .
     ed. Francis Lieber. Philadelphia: Lea & Blanchard, 1845-55.

     There is a brief summary of Wollstonecraft's life.

710 Holroyd, Maria Josepha. THE GIRLHOOD OF MARIA JOSEPHA HOL-
     ROYD. London: Longmans, Green and Co., 1896.

     A letter of 1795 mentions Wollstonecraft and A VINDICATION
     OF THE RIGHTS OF WOMAN. The observations in it are described
     as sensible and just.

711 LITERARY WORLD: A FORTNIGHTLY REVIEW OF CURRENT LITERATURE
     XV, 452-3.

     The review of Elizabeth Robins Pennell's LIFE OF MARY WOLL-
     STONECRAFT is entitled "A Rehabilitation of Mary Wollstone-
     craft." The book is described as an effort to brighten a
     tarnished name. The effort is considered unsuccessful, for
     the story of Wollstonecraft's life remains a painful and
     profitless one; it reveals the error of defying the moral
     sense of mankind.

712 Maunder, Samuel. THE BIOGRAPHICAL TREASURY: A DICTIONARY
OF UNIVERSAL BIOGRAPHY. London: Longmans, Green, and Co.,
1878.

An entry on Mary Wollstonecraft briefly sketches her life.
She appears also in the William Godwin entry, and here
Maunder refers to her masculine spirit and to the Godwins'
compatibility in matters of politics and morals.

713 Salt, Henry S. SHELLEY'S PRINCIPLES. HAS TIME REFUTED OR
CONFIRMED THEM? London: W. Reeves, 1892.

Henry Salt states that Shelley derived his ideas from many
writers, including Wollstonecraft.

1900 - 1975

714 Angeli, Helen R. SHELLEY AND HIS FRIENDS IN ITALY. London:
Methuen, 1911.

Comparisons are made between Wollstonecraft and her daughter,
Mary Shelley.

715 Antal, Frederick. FUSELI STUDIES. London: Routledge &
Kegan Paul, 1956.

In the notes there is reference to the relationship between
Wollstonecraft and Fuseli.

716 Bigland, Eileen. MARY SHELLEY. London: Cassell, 1959.

The first chapter provides a fairly full summary of Wollstonecraft's life.

717 Bouten, Jacob. MARY WOLLSTONECRAFT AND THE BEGINNING OF
FEMALE EMANCIPATION IN FRANCE AND ENGLAND. Amsterdam:
H. J. Paris, 1922.

Jacob Bouten relates Wollstonecraft to the feminist tradi-
tions of England and France. He discusses the difference
between Wollstonecraft and the Bluestockings.

718 Burdett, Osbert. WILLIAM BLAKE. New York: Macmillan Company, 1926.

There is mention of Wollstonecraft as one of the authors
published by Joseph Johnson.

719 CLEVELAND PLAIN DEALER, 31 August 1975.

This review of Jean Detre's A MOST EXTRAORDINARY PAIR dis-
cribes the work as a brilliantly imagined fiction and a
well researched biography. A summary of the Wollstonecraft-
Godwin relationship is given.

720 Glut, Donald F. THE FRANKENSTEIN LEGEND: A TRIBUTE TO MARY
SHELLEY AND BORIS KARLOFF. Metuchen, N. J.: Scarecrow Press,
1973.

Wollstonecraft is briefly mentioned. It is said that Godwin
never forgave his daughter for causing the death of Wollstonecraft.

721 Holmes, Richard. SHELLEY THE PURSUIT. New York: E. P. Dutton,
1975.

There are several mentions of Wollstonecraft as Godwin's first
wife, as a radical writer of the 1790s, and as a literary and
philosophical influence on Shelley.

722 McCloskey, Frank H. "Mary Shelley's Frankenstein," THE HUMANI-
TIES IN THE AGE OF SCIENCE: IN HONOR OF PETER SAMMARTINO.
Edited by Charles Angoff. Rutherford: Fairleigh Dickinson
University Press, 1968.

A short description of Wollstonecraft is given. Her untimely
death at her daughter's birth is said to have deprived the
child of the personal influence that such an intelligent and
courageous mother would have exerted.

723 Rosenberg, Samuel. "The Horrible Truth about Frankenstein,"
LIFE, 64, 11, March 1968, 74 - 84.

A short résumé of Wollstonecraft's life is given. It is
stated that Godwin felt his daughter should atone for having
caused her mother's death by replacing her intellectually.

724 Small, Christopher. MARY SHELLEY'S FRANKENSTEIN: TRACING THE
MYTH. Pittsburgh: University of Pittsburgh Press, 1972.

There is mention of Godwin's great grief at the loss of Wollstonecraft.

725 Thompson, E. P. "Solitary Walker," NEW SOCIETY, XIX, September 1974, 749-751.

In his review of Claire Tomalin's biography of Wollstonecraft,
E. P. Thompson objects to the inequitable treatment Wollstonecraft has received from historians and critics, who see her
less as a significant intellectual and moralist than as an
"Extraordinary Woman." In his opinion, they concentrate on
her personal crises to a far greater extent than they do on
the crises of men. Thompson finds Tomalin's biography disappointing, since it diminishes Wollstonecraft's stature and
condescends to her work.

726 Tomalin, Claire. "Mary Wollstonecraft and the Rights of Women,"
LISTENER, 87, January 1972, 77 - 79.

Claire Tomalin discusses the feminist theories of Wollstonecraft
and states that they were put into practice later but without

reference to her. Wollstonecraft's emphasis on a stable
home for children is noted; it is said to distinguish her
from some modern feminists who reject women's role as par-
ent and homemaker.

727 Wardle, Ralph M. THE WORDSWORTH CIRCLE, VI, 3, Summer 1975,
     147 - 150.

In his review of Claire Tomalin's LIFE AND DEATH OF MARY
WOLLSTONECRAFT, Ralph Wardle expresses his liking for the
new research undertaken for the book but his dislike of
Tomalin's disregard for exact detail and her use of Woll-
stonecraft's novels as histories of her life. He accuses
Tomalin of a tendency to turn a striking phrase at the cost
of strict accuracy and to indulge in disparaging gossip at
Wollstonecraft's expense.